LOVE & STRENGTH

BOOKS BY VALERIE HARPER

The Falcons Guard Collection
A Young Girl's Guide into a Self-Empowered Life
Finding Home
The Journey Into Self Understanding
Love & Strength
The Wounded Feminine
Love & Strength the Workbook
Creating Your Own Family
Falcons Guard the Foundation – Master Book

A Falcons Guard Collection

Love & Strength

A Parent's Guide to Raising Emotionally Intelligent Children

BOOK ONE OF EIGHT

Valerie Harper

A MOUNTAIN LOTUS PUBLICATION
SCOTTSDALE ARIZONA
2014

First U.S. Edition

Copyright © 2014 by Valerie Harper

ALL RIGHTS RESERVED

For information about permission to reproduce selections from this book, write to Permissions at mountainlotuspublications@gmail.com.

Library of Congress Catologin-in-Publication Data
Valerie Harper, date.

Love and strength: one of eight in Falcons Guard Collection / Valerie Harper. /
1st U.S. ed.
ISBN-0-9740827-08 (paperback)
India & Mexico

Printed in the United States of America

*For all of the people in this world
who make this world a better place
by showing children love*

FALCONS GUARD

A family system is how each member emotionally operates that makes up the whole system. When each family operates with emotional harmony individually, they can better function within the family and among society. Raising emotionally intelligent children comes from understanding key principles discussed in this book.

This book was written on behalf of Falcons Guard Center; an organization that promotes love and creativity. It is intended to be used as a guide to facilitate more socio-emotional growth for parents, children and families. Falcons Guard is dedicated to helping families gain more understanding in order to help their family systems function with more harmony. Falcons Guard Center has obtained the rights to use this book exclusively as their guide for parenting with greater emotional intelligence.

Please note that no person whatsoever is responsible for how you use this information including the publisher, author and anyone involved in the production of this book. Any and all suggestions made are intended for those of sound mind who take personal responsibility in choosing to raise their kids successfully. You can learn more about Falcons Guard classes by visiting www.FalconsGuardCenter.org.

Falcons Guard Center
Mesa, Arizona

Valerie Harper

Thank you for your purchase of this book.
Proceeds go to benefit the youth of
Falcons Guard Center.

Special thanks to: Dave Mietus,
Marianne Ferrari & Mary Moore

This book was independently written on behalf of Falcons Guard. The copyright is solely owned by the author. Falcons Guard Organization has obtained the legal right to use this book for educational purposes for their non-profit organization. Proceeds go to benefit their cause. No person, school, organization or group of individuals has the right to use, redistribute, reproduce or claim ownership over the material in anyway. Teaching rights require written and notarized permission from the author and publisher. Anyone in violation of copyright infringement laws as outlined in Chapter 5 § 501 Sections 106 through 122 106A(a) are subject to penalties as outlined in section § 506 for copyright infringement and will incur penalties for profits and damages. For information as to how you may use this material or how you may obtain teaching rights, contact the publishing house at MountainLotusPublications.com and the author at ValerieHarperConsulting.com

CONTENT

Foreward by Elizabeth Inganamort
12
Introduction Emotional Intelligence
15
Having the Right Support
23
Having a Child as a Rite of Passage
31
The Personality Forming
39
Love, Choices & Mating
43
Balanced Emotional Expressing
49
Creating the Framework for Good Parenting
55
Making Life Perfect
63
Behavior as Emotional Language
67
Emotional Wellness as a Parent
73
Remaining Emotionally Connected
81
The Seven Stages of Preparing Your Child for the Future
85
Being In Command of Your Family
91
Healthy Boundaries
97
Unexpected Journeys
101
Raising a Child in Abusive Conditions
105
Silent Power
109
Controlling Relationships
113
Family Dynamics
117
Unloving Relationships
119
Core Needs
125
Conclusion & Q & A
130-178

Foreward

My name is Elizabeth Inganamort. At 20 years old I was all by myself with an 8 month old baby and a 5 year old boy, both boys. I had just moved to the US as a legal immigrant but I didn't speak the language and I didn't have anything. I had no work, no money and no place to live. I had to follow my intuition. I think every mother has an intuition. Even animals have intuition to protect their child against anything. I had to follow my intuition to do everything and I grew up as a woman with children.

I trusted my intuition and began doing feng shui, which is the art of reading the energy in your environment to make your life better. That is when I found out I wasn't the only one with these unmet needs. People were having the same difficulties, especially women as mothers with their daughters because the parents think they know more. Or, they have bad relationships with each other that are disrespectful.

What I found was teens and mothers were not listening to each other. Teens have feelings too because they have to grow. They have to find their own way in life. Sometimes if you just support them they get along better than if you are always fighting them. When parents fight their kids they run away and get into bad company. They sometimes get involved in drugs, sometimes prostitution, whatever. The girls leave the house for anything because they can't stand to being at home. Now they are robbing and acting bad because there is a rejection. They are misunderstandings and so they leave. I wanted to help all of these people but couldn't individually. I began to dream of a way that I could make this happen.

While I had my feng shui business I had a radio show talking about colors and how they can change the moods of people, especially kids. The callers started confusing energy with psychology. I would tell them everything is about energy but I had to stop because I wasn't a counselor but people were asking about all of this stuff. I felt the emergency to start helping them by myself. A couple of years ago I met Valerie.

We began working together. She is a healer. She communicates what I know in my heart but don't always have English words for. One of the people I had taken in as a legal guardian was very rebellious. She didn't want to talk to Valerie but after she did, she liked Valerie. She has also helped me with my own healing. She has helped many people and that is why I asked her to write this book for Falcons Guard. I think everyone should have this book in their home.

I want to help teens in crisis. I want to help mothers and daughters. I figure many will be the cause but few will be the one who chooses to act on the vision. I chose to act on my vision.

To me, there is a state of emergency between teens and their parents. What I see are girls that need a lot of help. I see girls who would do anything to be on T.V. and do anything to be noticed when there is no need. I had to take the teens that ask me for help and take them into my house. I had to take them under my roof and give them food.

I know this book is going to help you understand your child. You are going to be a parent forever and you will have to know how to parent them until they can leave home. This book will help you heal so you can be a better parent. We have to be good role models. We have to give something to our kids. Kids become the fruit of our parenting. I hear a lot of people say my mother was an alcoholic or my grandfather beat me up. If people can't find the love they need then they come to the center to find it. We will make sure the people who are working there have good hearts.

Too many times even good parents allow their kids to go out alone and figure it out before giving them the proper tools. At

18 some kids are not ready. They are scared. They are like a new baby out in the world. You think that when your baby is wearing diapers they are ready but they are scared. They have to work and go to school. This is when they need the most support. But no, we leave them alone. They start using drugs. We find them dead on the streets of the school because they are drunk. I want to see a big change. There is no need for any of this to be happening.

We have many opportunities at Falcons Guard to get involved. We invite you to participate, donate and attend our events and buy our products and services. All proceeds go to help our vision of creating the world's largest loving home that takes in children. Your kids need you. At Falcons Guard we provide support for parents too. It is for everyone, not just troubled youth. We look forward to receiving your contributions to help make this world a better place.

I am 100 percent devoted and committed to my purpose. I have three beautiful boys; Jorge, William and Jake. It is my children who have inspired me to start Falcons Guard. They teach me so much about who I am and life. It is beautiful to find out my purpose. I want to teach the kids in this world how to find respect for who they are.

Sincerely,
Elizabeth Inganamort

Valerie Harper

Introduction:
Emotional Intelligence

Being a parent can be extra challenging when you don't have the skills you need to properly deliver the love and strength it takes to be a good parent. When you have a difficult time managing your emotions it can come out in your caretaking.

This book is intended for people who would like to heal their emotional issues so that they can become a better parent. It will help you learn how to manage your own emotions so you can heal from your own childhood while effectively becoming the parent you are capable of being.

This book can also be used as a means to help prepare you for parenthood. Even if you are not a parent, people who read it find it to be beneficial for healing the harm that was done to them from their own upbringings.

There is a reason why people have emotional responses. Emotions are the energy that moves a person from a state of feeling into a state of action. Emotional intelligence comes from knowing what to do with these responses.

Your feelings have so much to tell you. Raising your child with emotional intelligence means you are allowing them to remain connected to the deepest part of themselves for life's navigation. When people have stored pain they can't access their higher wisdom of intelligence as easily. They act on defenses. These same emotional defenses come out in how a person parents. When you can move past this pain and get to the real emotional intelligence then you create a framework for success in your life and in your parenting.

Being a parent can be emotionally challenging. The role of being a caretaker requires so much love and strength that people can have a difficult time knowing how to respond to their own emotional needs as well as their children's needs. The extenuating circumstances that can take place in life can either add to the pressures of parenting. When you know how to manage emotional power you can make life a happier experience.

Financial difficulties will most likely add pressure for anyone. A loving partner or good friend can ease the tension but may not resolve the core problem. Emotional parenting requires a whole person and yet it is a process that is always evolving. It is important to accept where you are while simultaneously growing.

Regretting where you have been only causes more stagnation. Many people are parenting from their emotional wounds rather than from their pure essence of love. This book is intended to help you to do your inner work so you can set aside your problems, overcome your fears and have fun while being the best parent.

When you can approach parenting from a place of compassion and love, which can only come from having emotional intelligence, it makes parenting more enjoyable. You will still have challenges but you will have more ability to know how to manage your feelings. This kind of happiness will allow you to take care of your responsibilities while engaging fully with your family.

Your ability to raise an emotionally intelligent child comes from your own level of self-awareness. When a person is aware of who they are and what is actually taking place around them, they can act more mindfully. We can know what our emotional triggers are by the way we are responding to life. If there is an emotional trigger, then it needs to be recognized. There is either stored pain, or it is an indicator telling you something needs to be acted upon.

Everyone in a family is growing psychologically at the same time but in a different way emotionally. Each individual is experiencing something different while sharing the same moments simultaneously. This is why it is important to be mindful of how you are emotionally connected to your child.

When you are aware of your feelings you can be more mindful of what others are feeling as well. As you pay more attention to your emotional responses and how your children emotionally respond, you can become more vigilant as to what you allow into your home which will help you protect the people you care about.

By healing your own emotional wounds, you ensure that you are being the best parent you can be instead of someone who is parenting destructively. Humans operate from mental programs that are called beliefs. These beliefs develop throughout your own upbringing. Because the mind is always gathering information and computing what is happening, beliefs are always changing. These mental commands become automatic system of behavior and to a large extent, determine why people behave the way they do.

The world of psychology explains myriad behaviors based on mental programs. Your child has a set of beliefs they are operating from based on the experiences they have gone through. Their expressions come from their feelings based on what they are believing. When you raise an emotionally intelligent child these beliefs help them navigate life, positively.

The goal in emotionally intelligent parenting is to leave the five main functions of the self intact. When children do not get the emotional love or connection they need they suffer from emotional problems. They start to separate from their main functions and develop emotional defenses. This causes them to struggle in life rather than to flourish. When parents take the time to commit to positive emotional exchanges that should take place on a daily basis, they decrease the chances for mental problems occurring.

Living with unresolved emotions of hurt, loss, hardship or any traumatic experiences is painful. Parents have their own wounds that get passed on if they are not emotionally mindful. These wounds can continue on for generations leaving legacies in families that will affect the way each person parents. Your overall success as a parent is determined by how you manage stress. Taking emotional inventory can assist you in acting more mindfully so you can have positive and fulfilling connections with your offspring instead of connections riddled with difficulty.

People manage stress in a variety of different ways. People form addictions when they can't find relief. They seek relationships that may not be good for them. They also suppress their feelings to avoid conflict. All of these coping mechanisms are ineffective for bringing about true happiness.

All parents handle stress differently. You can see the difference in kids who have parents that emotionally freak out on their kids, versus the ones who take the time to communicate effectively.

Parents who don't enjoy parenting become checked out and removed from all involvement as a way of coping. A parent who holds everything inside and never says anything may do so because they do not know how to set effective boundaries. They end up affecting their kids due to this deficiency. We are all connected and always learning about the people we are with. It is important to take the time to be mindful about life and develop emotional intelligence.

The emotional states you hold affect your parenting. Learning how to engage comes from being balanced emotionally. This means they know who they are and how they are feeling. They have the capacity to interact emotionally based on other people's emotionality. People who enjoy parenting are operating from a high level of intelligence emotionally.

There is a specific way of achieving emotional intelligence. This book will give you the tools and inner resources you need to start living a more fulfilling life as a parent. At first paying attention to your feelings might feel awkward but in the end the process will be very rewarding.

The shift from unconscious parenting into emotionally intelligent parenting begins with knowing what you are feeling in every moment. When you are connected to your feelings you are connected to your truth. Accessing your truth comes from being willing to enter your emotional power. Your emotional power comes from knowing how you feel in every moment without having to take it out on anyone. When you enter your power a whole world of opportunities begins to open up. Relationships start to work, money starts to flow in and you can find the people in your family happy because they are allowed to operate from their true self.

Your overall success as a parent is determined by how you prepare your children for life. When you prepare your children for life using emotionally intelligence, the result is a happier world. People can see unhappiness anywhere they go. Unhappiness is nothing more than people not feeling what they are really feeling. People who have unfelt feelings don't know how to find their joy because they are living with emotional ignorance. This leads to poverty, destruction and more stress.

All healing begins with knowing your own home within. When you're at home with your feelings it doesn't matter where you go in life, you can be happy. Your home is found within.

Children are naturally connected to their feelings. The disconnection occurs when people train them to disconnect from their feelings by rejecting them or punishing them. Children learn what they can or cannot feel based on how they treat them. Raising a child with emotional intelligence means you can relate emotionally to what they are saying and you choose to interact with them. As you find your own connection to your emotional intelligence, you teach your child how to remain connected to their emotional intelligence so they can feel at home with themselves.

1

Healthy Societies Have a Network for Good Parental Support

In today's society people don't always have the love and support they need. There is a lot of competition that can lead to feelings of anxiety. This competitiveness takes place in our schools, churches and any social structures.

Competition is healthy when it's used to bring out the best in people. However, with the advancement of technology in modern lives, people might seem more connected but they have also become more preoccupied with multi-tasking during connection.

The fuller a person's life gets, the less people take time for wholesome activities. The more success a person strives for the more relationships and family diminishes in quality. Replacing relationships with goals does something to a person.

Humans thrive on healthy intimacy. When people don't get the intimacy they need, they shut down emotionally. This breakdown of emotional connection leads to a unhappiness at the deepest level.

Dysfunction is defined by the inability to healthily relate to other individuals emotionally. When there is dysfunction in a family or society, members can easily confuse their roles and start operating separate from what is in their own best interest. Children may be acting like the adult or violently trying to survive their youth. They may be exposed to unhealthy attitudes that make them closed off to others.

A family living in fear might separate from other people in society, and that may limit the childrens' growth. Sometimes the seclusion is healthier than having unhealthy connections. Yet in the long run, it always affects happiness. Depending how society responds to someone it may influence how willing that person is to engage within the social system.

Anytime a family loses connection to a healthy social network their emotional health will be affected. This will include the loss of a parent, sibling or any loss within their social structure.

People are social beings and we have to have social connection to thrive. Success in life has to do with our circumstances in life and our quality of connections. When the relationship dynamics of a family are diminished or dysfunctional, it compromises the social connection of an individual.

More people are becoming single parents and raising kids alone. This causes extra exposure to potential problems. Other people have multiple partnerships that influence the emotional challenges that rise up for their kids.

Socially, the family structure is changing substantially to where the lines that distinguish parent from child have been blurred in some cases. This blurring of roles is causing a lot of extra challenges for kids. Children need to know who they are, where they fit in and that they are wanted. If they have to take on a different role other than just being a kid then it causes stress. This stress can only be alleviated by having healthy social connections and a solid network of good people who play their role.

A teacher that becomes a lover plays a confusing role. A parent who isn't parenting makes it difficult for a child to know who they can turn to for support. Without good, trustworthy friends, family and affiliations there is social pain they have to deal with.

What good parents realize is that kids have their own stress. They know they need to take the time to help them emotionally process. Children can actually have more stress than adults because they don't have coping skills to handle their emotions. When they look for outlets of expression but get rejected, they shut down.

Children look to their parents to give them the social cues they need to handle their relationships. Many parents that have kids don't even know how to handle their own adult relationships. This poses a problem for this younger generation's level of success and happiness.

To really love your child into adulthood they need a complexity of loving relationships. They need a mother who provides nurturance and care. They need a father who provides protection and love. They need siblings they feel safe with. They need friends they can relate to. They need teachers who believe in them. They need a social structure that allows them to thrive. They need a sense of spirituality and understanding of the deeper realms of life. They even need a sense of meaning as to why they are living their lives, which means they also need a sense of direction as to where they're going.

A missing sense of purpose seems to be the number one thing that's missing for children, today—a passion for the direction in which they feel themselves moving. Their sense of purpose is missing and everyone needs a sense of purpose to feel happy.

When people live without passion there is nothing driving them. Passion is the fuel for success. Passion can only come from being connected to one's feelings. The most valuable thing you can do as a parent for your child is to find your own passions. Remain connected to your feelings and include them in all of your visions.

When you succeed while balancing all other responsibilities, it does something even greater for your whole family. When you achieve your success and follow through with acknowledgment and recognition for their contributions, something even greater happens.

Everyone plays an integral role in the success of a family. Your children need to have their own passions. Notice what they are drawn to and how their passions are different than yours. When you can recognize what their passions are, you can better support them by being the emotional mirror that reflects these passions back to them.

Your overall skills as a parent are determined by the level of interdependence your children experience while growing up. At first, they will be totally dependent on you in every way. If you constantly respond to their each and every need when they arrive you will have a happier child inside. The stronger the social network of people they have in their life the more they will thrive.

As they grow they will develop physical, emotional and mental autonomy. This independence is continuously developing. They become their own person each and every year when they are allowed the freedom to operate independently. The freedom to be who they are comes from a parent who operates interdependently. This means the parent allows their child to rely on them where needed until they are operating fully.

When you have healthy relationships in your life, your child gets to practice being in a relationship. If you as parent are too controlling or overbearing, then your child doesn't have the chance to develop full autonomy. They might even become independent and rebellious, but in a way that emerges out of resistance.

When a person acts from counter-resistance, they usually make choices that really don't serve them. Emotional resistance comes from a conflict of power. Each individual in life should be able to make their own choices in and about life because it is in the healthy interdependence that makes a person thrive.

Allowing your child to make their own choices is what gives them their faculties that are essential for life. Interdependence is the ability to be who you are independent of who another person is while still being able to engage in a healthy and positive interaction.

An unhealthy relationship is always based on power and control or a complete lack of self that allows for other people to walk all over the person who isn't in their power. People who lack emotional intelligence don't know how to relate or interact with other people. They are either all inward or emotionally all over the place. Having healthy emotional intelligence naturally creates a rapport for positive interactions with others. It is what is developed through a positive social network.

Healthy interdependence can only be achieved within a group that allows for interdependent interactions. Parents who cannot connect to their children due to the difference of opinions, lose emotional connection. When connection is lost it opens up your child to anyone they are exposed to.

You are their leader when they are young. You have the first chance to program them with the right information. If you wait to show them what they need to know, they will miss out because they won't be properly informed. If you are not there emotionally leading them, other people will come in and take advantage of the. Especially, if they are not fully developed or still in the stages of dependence.

Emotionally vacant parents can love their kids but miss the clues that someone is abusing them. It is through a lost emotional connection that allows other people to access your child and start abusing them.

An emotionally healthy person has no need to abuse anyone. They are in their power and they don't need to steal the emotional power from anyone. When there is a lack of intelligence on how to relate, there are other things that start to come up for the child such as social difficulties and low self-esteem. You as a parent need to be as healthy as you can to be so you can emotionally respond to what they are experiencing through their own sensations and feelings. Your role as a parent is to be the "practice" relationship for them. They should be able to voice their opinions but in a way that is respectful. They should have a voice but still have to listen.

Freedom of your child's voice power is essential for life. Having a voice means they can communicate, be heard and receive feedback that what they said was registered and made a difference. When there is no relationship to catch their emotional expression and mirror it back for them, feelings stay stuck. The part of them that wants to be heard isn't being received. Kids turn to drugs, overeating and complacency when they cannot find a release for what they're feeling. Having the right relationships, in life, helps your child interact in a way that builds emotional self-awareness. This comes from listening to what they are saying.

You are the best person to help your child know who they are. You are there to reflect back to them all the wonderful qualities that make them who they are. If you are a controlling parent and feel the need to cut away at your kids in an attempt to eliminate anything that you find unpleasant, you will cause harm to them. They need to know that you genuinely love them. If they don't feel this love then they will grow up believing they are flawed.

Some parents can control via horrible and constant criticisms, cutting their kids down to eliminate parts of them that lead to them feeling ashamed of who they are, for no reason other than their own neurotic feelings of self-doubt. Control limits emotional expression. It rejects and denies another person leaving them feel inadequate and frustrated. This is really unfair to do to someone. Criticism never works and it's a violation of the self.

Your child will not know their worth until you show them. Finding emotionally intelligent ways to give constructive feedback is what a good parent does. Your child needs you as their mirror, not for constant criticism. Just give feedback as to what you see within them. Eliminate all opinions which only emotionally entangles them. Reflect back to them what they are saying by validating their underlying feelings. Take time to evaluate the full relationship.

Consider the quality of emotional connection you have with your child. Is it positive, or riddled with conflict? How might you begin to step into your own voice power and set boundaries you might need to set? Evaluate if you have enough people in your life that support you. Emotional intelligence for you as a parent comes from having a positive network of people who love and support you and your kids, too.

To be a highly evolved civilization there must be huge amounts of awareness for the psychological operations that emerge as the result of individual life experiences. Who your child becomes is a result of how you criticize them and how you love them. Be discretionary when you think to put them down. Your influence is powerfully forming them.

Valerie Harper

2

Having a Child Is a Rite of Passage

There is nothing more exciting than finding out you are going to have a baby, especially when the conditions are right. But who knows when the conditions are right?

The event of bringing another human being into the world is typically very exciting. You have waited a long time for this special person and they are finally arriving. The moment you see your baby you have an emotional response to what is happening. You gave birth to this person. Or, you have observed the birth of this person. Either way, this is nothing short of a miracle.

The body is miraculous and so is the evolution of the parenting process. People might forget how amazing it is because the process of raising a child versus growing a baby is slowed down and extended out over time. Instead of 9 months, you have about 216 months or 18 years. And what happens in each year is very important.

The story of your child's life is unfolding and you as the parent or guardian are their main supporting character. The events that play out for your child are directly related to the events and choices you make throughout your life. Having a baby is a rite of passage. It moves you into a different stage of your own experience. It signifies an emotional milestone.

What parents don't always realize is the outcome of their children is an overall reflection of what they were exposed to overtime. Parents can be very hard on themselves. The truth is, everything in life is a process. Your baby arrives and it's a process. You try to breastfeed and they are unable to latch on. It's a process. Your child becomes a teenager and now you have to deal with their attitude. It is all a process. Your child is old enough to leave home and doesn't. Life is one big evolutionary process. There is a learning curve that must always be managed. They start to grow and there is more to manage. The outcome is shaped by who you become and your awareness. You have to be so keyed into life that you don't overlook anything.

When you have a child with someone, often times it forges your energy together. You generally take on the energy of their family, friends and anything else that's woven into their lives. These people in your life become like a mini community that influences you emotionally. Love and support are essential to healthy families.

All healthy families have one thing in common. Each member plays an integral role in healthy interactions. If you have a relationship with your child that is contentious and volatile everyone will need to learn how to communicate their feelings in a more constructive way in order for the entire family to be more successful.

If you have a relationship with your spouse or significant other that doesn't support you, then your role as a parent will be compromised. Who you are linked to influences your parental qualities greatly. Everything in life affects the way you parent but especially your close, interpersonal relationships.

The more dysfunctional the family dynamics are the more difficult it is for you to navigate your way to good parenting through emotional awareness. Some of these relationships can become so unhealthy that you may even wonder why you even maintain them. Some parental obligations force us to remain in certain dynamics. However, there is always a way that you can overcome these challenges simply by the way you handle yourself through emotional intelligence.

The truth is, you are always free. No matter what you're doing in your life you are always free. You are free to be a good parent and you are always free to leave. You can choose to beat your kids or be caring. The choices you automatically make without thinking comes from who you are, emotionally.

A person with a wounded heart will almost always behave in an emotionally removed or destructive way. An unloving person who has hate in their heart will almost always inflict their pain onto another person in attempt to relieve their own pain. A parent who abandons their child does so because they can't handle the emotional responsibilities position. There are numerous dynamics and conditions that lead to emotional abandonment of anyone. When a parent abandons a child it is usually because they are too wounded for that time being to handle the responsibilities. After all, it is hard to expect someone who is emotionally wounded to adequately care for another person when typically they have a hard enough time caring for themselves.

Everyone in life has free will. What you choose to do as a parent will be up to you. If you choose to parent with more emotional intelligence there will be things you can heal in you. Your choices will always affect what your children do. When a person is connected to their heart, love is all they can express.

If you are a parent that chooses to leave your child, then you won't get any of the benefits that come from rearing them. If you abandon your child either emotionally, physically or financially, you may alleviate temporary responsibility but in the years to come it will create a lot of pain for yourself emotionally.

One of the many benefits of being proactive in the rearing of your child or children is how they mirror back to you aspects of who you really are. You get to see who you are emotionally by the way you show up with them in this relationship. You also get to see who you are through the different set of relational dynamics. This is what makes being a parent an interesting challenge. You get to manage all that is taking place around you as you attempt to parent.

Valerie Harper

There is no perfect utopia-like state when building your family. All you can do is your best. The current dynamics you find yourself in are all a part of your life. You can complain about what exists or you can get right down to it and triumph no matter what is a part of your experience.

When you parent with an open heart you might still make mistakes but at least you know your heart was in it. People who neglect to parent their kids when they are kids are known to experience a lot of regret.

There are some things that we cannot prevent such as parenting long distance. Sometimes your kids will be far away and yet there are always to stay connected no matter what type of grief you might be receiving from the other parent or other extenuating circumstances. No matter how much you dislike who you parent with, always revere your child because they are completely innocent.

A parent can either stay in touch or separate with or without being in close proximity to their child. An emotionally distant parent gets to see who they are too. There are always ways of staying connected to your children no matter how far removed you have become. Your relationship with your child is cumulative. The quality of your connection is measured by the quality of every moment you spend with them. Love them. Be there for them and participate in their growth.

Sometimes remaining connected to the child is difficult when the caregiving parent is constantly abusing the absent parent. A parent may choose to leave in order to avoid the constant barrage of attacks. These dynamics become more complicated with each case and yet there are ways to work through them.

When a person is connected to their heart, love is all they can express. Parents who use their kids as power objects are really out of touch with their love. They have usually yet to develop the personal power they need to allow another person their own free will. Power plays usually come from parents who are emotionally wounded and can't connect emotionally to others. They use power plays to get what they want and end up exploiting others to control the situation. These are people who are not operating from, nor do they possess, either emotional integrity or truth. A person who is in their power only wants to operate from the highest standards of integrity and truth.

Working through these dynamics gets complicated and yet anything can be worked through. It's about holding your power and being the best you.

A good parent knows they have the responsibility to govern their life in a direction that will support themselves and their children. When a parent misses out on such an opportunity, there is a loss. Emotionally intelligent people always choose to be loving and act on behalf of the good of the whole. They create a winning formula for everybody or as close as possible. A parent may have to do whatever they have to do to survive but it is important to remain emotionally connected to good people or else there will be emptiness inside.

There is a deep need within all parents to fully be there for their child even if they cannot adequately care for them. Who you are caring for is dependent on your love for their quality of life. If you are a parent that suffers from chronic lying, addictions, or narcissism it is important to seek help.

Then there are imbalances that come from parents who devote every ounce of who they are into being a parent. They leave little to not time for themselves. If you live to give your child everything, you will lose meaning in your own life. Overachieving parents eventually burnout. The challenge of a caring parent comes from knowing how to navigate the intricate balance of caretaking with care of the self.

Always seek balance. If you put in the time when your kids need you the most they will be able to live their lives on their own. If you over give and over care-take, you will find your life empty once they are gone. You can devote all you are to your family but always create a portion of your life that is your own.

Parents today seem to think being able to give their kids everything they need and want makes them a great parent. Parents who give their kids everything without making them resourceful hunters and gatherers at life, raise inept kids who are unprepared for surviving life. Every child should have appropriate responsibilities both physically and emotionally, but at the right developmental stage they are in so they can emotionally handle it. How you handle doling out responsibilities will affect their attitude towards basic tasks.

Parents can make the mistake in believing that emotional intelligence means allowing their kids to behave any way they want. They may even think it is cruel to set healthy guidelines. Children are not meant to be coddled their whole lives. They are meant to be loved and coddled from the beginning and then it tapers off. They become independent individuals that you then champion them into their own unique paths. You are the parent. They are yours to raise into fully functioning young adults. All success comes with balance.

Parents who coddle their children despite the child's attempts to strike out on their own, can make kids believe they are inept to take their places in society. Some kids become huge followers when this happens. Others become too afraid to achieve their dreams or leave home permanently.

Parents are to coddle their children entirely until the age of two or three. Then they are to still care for them after their child has at least attempted the situation independently. By teenagers they are to be self-sufficient to a large degree. Anymore, parents are buying their adult kids condos to live in rent free. What does this teach? This is coddling. Caring for a child's emotional well-being isn't.

Allowing your adult child to live in your home or condo rent free for an allotted amount of time can be appropriate if your child just experienced something devastating. It can be a sign of love and not coddling. It all depends on the circumstances and what they are or are not doing.

What you, as a successful parent wants, is to impart is the message that you believe in your child, and make them believe in themselves. Their belief should be enough that they then believe they can do what they set their mind to. You are there to support them, not indulge them in an over protective way. This will make them love and appreciate you even more because of how you it empowers them to know what to do.

There is a lot to gain from the experience of parenting. It is a very natural thing to do. Having a baby satisfies something deep inside of us. It connects us to that place that resides deep within. This is where the most primitive aspects of the self are found. It is also from this place where you find the source of joy that comes from the effort you put into raising your children.

Having a baby means something. You are creating from your soul. You have brought a child into this world to have an experience. You are willing to give of yourself in order for your child to have an opportunity to live and experience life. This is satisfying to the soul at the deepest level. No matter how challenging the experience may be at times, it is deeply gratifying. Access this emotional level and you will develop a different relationship to the challenges parenting poses.

The challenges that come with parenting provide opportunities for your own soul to grow. Your child has so much to teach you and you are willing because there is so much love. Many people find babies absolutely amazing because they are beautiful little creations of pure energy. As they grow they are still this continuous bundle of love and potentiality. You are shaping who they are as they grow. This can be simultaneously intimidating and exciting. How you navigate the challenges influence your children's entire upbringing.

To some parents the idea of being emotionally responsible for their kids is terrifying. They put their lives on hold to make sure they parent perfectly. This is probably the worst thing you could do for yourself long term. You don't have to wait for your kids to grow up to find your happiness. You can find happiness right now just by reconnecting to this present moment. This isn't easy when you are responsibly caretaking. When you can care take, manage your life, take time for yourself and still keep your cool, then you are operating as the most evolved parent.

All of life is a process. When you flow with it, everything happens naturally. You will find your way to true happiness. Just stay awake through each stage of the process.

Being awake is the only way to create the life you want. Being "awake" means paying attention to what is really happening. Admit the truth of what is really happening within your family. Come to terms with losses or difficult parts of the journey. Avoid living in fantasy. Your life is what it is right now. Observe it. If you don't like it, change it.

What you do as a parent comes from doing what is best for yourself. The happier you are, the better off they are as long as you remember their life is developing as you go. If you make choices only to suit them you have already forgotten the most important person leading who is in charge of this process. When you are educated about the parenting process, you can make more informed choices that benefit you, your child and everyone involved within the overall dynamics.

3

Personality Developing

Some people believe when a child is born, much of their personality tendencies are already preformed. Your parenting skills are going to give them what they intellectually know. Deep down they already have their own personality and tendencies based on their own unique path in life. You may look at your child and wonder how they are going to be 20 years from the moment they were born. The answer to this is perfect! They will be absolutely who they are meant to be if you just love them.

When you meet your child for the first time you are learning all about them. You will be doing this many times over and over as they grow. The very first time your child thinks and expresses their own cognitive thought can be very exciting. It means their sense of self developing. When this first occurs you are now communicating with this cognitive self. This occurs around the ages of four to five. When your child reaches this certain cognitive stage their fears will begin surfacing. What your child fears by the time they are 5 will affect them for the rest of their life.

What kids are trying to do at this age is to try to figure out life. They want to know if life is safe? They want to know if they have the permission to respond naturally. They see what happens to other people who don't behave accordingly and it creates in their mind a concept of who they should be.

It is important for your children to perceive life accurately. If they are to be emotionally intelligent, feeding into fictitious events might be recognized as fun but one has to contemplate what fantasy actually is does to them?

Around the age of 5 is also they start to question life and what it means to live or die. Some of their responses may not make sense but there is always a good reason as to why they are responding the way they are. They can have a lot of fears but not know why. If they have the vocabulary they will be able to express these feelings. If they don't have the words or the understanding they will act out the fear or the feelings behaviorally.

You as a parent help them when you state what you are seeing without criticizing or blaming. You can always tell what a child is feeling by the way they are behaving. When they get a little older they may withhold expressions making reading them a little more challenging. As your child gets older you can rely on external indicators to tell you what they are feeling such as the cleanliness of their bedroom to the friends they choose. If their quality of their hygiene then they are usually not feeling so good about themselves.

Kids are feeling a lot of things. They are always giving their parents clues as to what is happening internally. The question becomes, are you as the parent listening and interpreting the signs accurately?

Parenting is a close emotional union. A child is express what a parent is feeling but not saying. All behavior can be linked to the parent and vice versa. A child's emotions affect the parent just as much which is why it is so important for everyone to have their emotional rhythms.

The healthier you show up no matter what their behavior is the less they have to take on certain behaviors as defensive. While they are developing their own personalities you can still do the things that you need to feel good. Be mindful that every thought you think and every feeling you express is rooted in love.

Sometimes you have to discuss real hard issues but when you do so with respect for everyone then you are coming from a place of emotional intelligence. Being mindful of how you communicate means every time you enter the connection for communication it is done with the intent to love and not just to vent what is wrong.

Your child's development depends on you. There are certain things they need to be able to leave home and live without you. There will be losses and triumphs along the way. The key to successful parenting is being open to who they are continuously becoming. Your children are always changing in their own ways. The more you love and support them in their growth the better they feel. Your love for them is expressed when you reveal genuine aspects of yourself that are real.

We treat our kids the way we treat ourselves. The way we learned to treat ourselves is the way others treated us. Are you treating your child the way you would want to be treated or the way you are used to being treated?

4

Love, Choices & Mating

Life is complex. People find out the importance of who they sleep with after they have already mated. Most people don't always understand the full ramifications of their choices. What you do from here is defined by the next series of choices you make.

There is a lot that goes into selecting the right person to have a baby with. Some people leave their mating choices up to chance. They operated on chemistry alone instead of combining it with a little intellect. This can give way to a totally unforeseen set of experiences that are all perfect within the grander scheme of things.

Who you mate with will impact the rest of our life. It is singlehandedly the most important decision that will affect the course of your parental life. Some people don't realize this and end up gambling on love that influences the rest of their lives and their kid's lives. No matter who you choose to mate with, that choice will always affect others around you.

Who you have a child with makes a makes a world of difference in your overall experience. The relationship you are in foreshadows your emotional state as a parent. If you mate with a narcissist you will have to contend with their selfishness. If you mated with an alcoholic you will have to contend with their inability to have a relationship with anything other than their substance and whatever emotional pains they cover up by getting drunk. If you mated with a workaholic you may have a lot of money but not a lot of time to be with this person. If you mated with a chronic liar you will have to contend with the lack of trust in your life. If you mated with a healthy, balanced emotionally available breadwinner that takes pride in their efforts you will have an easier path, provided that you're not in love with someone else. The partner you parent frames the entire experience.

There is always something to learn from every choice that is made and yet some consequences just were not considered. Whatever the extenuating circumstances that you found yourself in when you conceived automatically become a part of your child's experience. Either way, you have the responsibility of caring for this amazing person you brought into this world even if you conceived through a sexual violation. There is something exceptionally unique about this child. There may be a lot of emotions you have to contend with first before you can parent full heartedly when situations like this arise. However, the more love you have for this child the more it reflects how powerful you are. There is no other experience like this one. Your child is this amazingly unique combination that you may or may not fully understand. Your role is to love them no matter what and work to understand them. They are going to challenge you every step of the way. Your job is to love them and give them the best possible structure for growth you can.

With the intimate roles you are playing you will most likely know your child better than anyone. You are their guardian. You are to respect and honor them. The more respect they receive from the beginning, the better chance they have at growing up to be a remarkable person. You are going to raise them, love them and be there for them, not to take away their problems but to teach them how to navigate problems. Life is a series of challenges making it nothing but navigating through conflict. The better you are at navigating conflict the more you have to teach them. You shape who they are. You know their likes, their dislikes along with their fears and insecurities. They look to you for the reassurance they are okay. Give it to them. You are their world. Without your reassurance they won't feel safe to explore. Kids need this at every stage. The more faith you have in them the more they learn they can do anything.

As a parent, if you reject your child because of who you mated with, you are only rejecting the part of yourself that the child represents. You will never remove your seed from that child. Your seed goes on, and what you do determines what happens within him, too. This is why when a parent loses a child to abuse or kidnapping their soul gets ripped out.

What happens to your child happens to you. Love that child as if they are you. Give them whatever they need and see them through. Don't over give in their latter years because just like you, they wish to become successful and powerful too. If you over care they never learn to do what they need to do. The key is finding the emotional balance in whoever you have a child with even if they are nothing like you. Love is still accepting them even if you don't want them close to you. You can accept they are cold and heartless, or however you would describe your experience with them, and then shower your child with the love you have inside from all the peace of mind you gain through that acceptance.

Spending time on emotional resentments occurs because people feel they suffered a violation. If you find yourself holding onto resentments towards your child's other parent, it is most likely due to feeling violated because the results were not what you had expected. You connected with this person for a reason. No matter who this person is they hold some level of value as a human. No matter how abusive or uncaring they may have been to you, there is still value they brought you when they brought in a child. You have a precious gift you get to tend to.

When you feel injustice for who you mated with, feel what you feel and allow the emotions to wash through you. There is nothing you have to do except stand in your truth. If you are unhappy with who you mated with, the truth is you still have a job to do. Feel what you feel and find a way to move through what happened with you. The child doesn't care who their parent is. They are just happy to be here having their set of experiences too. Love them and be grateful no matter who mated with you. When you resolve all of your feelings you will feel grateful for having them too.

When selecting a mate be sure to use both your intellect and emotional intelligence. Choosing a mate on chemistry alone may turn out to be an unfulfilling relationship. There are many key ingredients that make a mate a perfect fit. Have kids with someone who values you and your parental role.

As humans we thrive on love. We are here because of love and we continue to live from receiving love. If you are a parent that was depleted of love in your youth than you probably mated while looking for love that may or may not have come through. Any unfelt emotions stored from the past will affect you. They will unconsciously influence your choices and what you do. Some people find they need to go back and re-parent themselves to get to a more honest place. They need to know what happened in their childhood that made them this way. Often times, this self-reflection is confusingly complex. There are so many little things that impact a person that it is hard to pinpoint what specifically. Most people find self-healing productive as long as they remain connected to present day reality. What people need to know most is they can heal anything. When they give themselves permission to feel they give themselves the ability to heal.

Your fears contour your parenting process. There are fears involved with any responsibility. None are as important as caring for an individual properly. Self-help books teach how to reshape the self, using a variety of methods for letting go of trauma caused by parents. This movement has caused parents to become extra cautious to not over traumatize their child but leaves the parent feeling like a parental co-dependent. There are all these ambiguous fears of wrecking the child.

It's important to know people are resilient. At any moment a person's psyche can be restored when they are honest with themselves. The more honest you are as a parent the better your child can grow. Teaching false theories thinking their life will be easier isn't so. Kids that are in denial spend their whole lives in fantasy. This doesn't mean come crashing down with some hard, cold reality. There is much to love about life when people do the work, what makes life the best is the love and understanding that comes from others.

There will be many opportunities to go back and self-reflect while parenting. After all, it is primarily your past set of experiences that is driving your parenting. Resolving the past conflicts allows you to feel more complete allowing you to feel more confident giving your child the adequate love, guidance and approval that they need. Any unhealed emotional wounds will come up in your parenting are usually triggered at the same age you were when your child gets there. Observe who you are as a parent as if you are in third person. Identify the things you do that may or may not be working. Are your behaviors contributing to a peaceful interaction or the past emotions getting acted out in ways that harm other people. Find a way to release negativity other than taking it out on people directly. There are specific things you can do to heal yourself and your family.

Start healing your family by founding all communication on appropriate levels of mental and emotional honesty. You know you have found appropriate level of emotional honesty when everyone is functioning well and happy. Expressing too much is like an emotional dump. The effect is similar to emotional withholding. Too much information is overwhelming. Find balance in how you express your truth by the emotional response you get from others.

Every person defines *love* differently. Sometimes love actually means giving someone their space and not touching them. Sometimes it is not complimenting them or telling them how cute or adorable they are. Love is ultimately the ability to recognize where someone is emotionally and allowing them the space to be where they are.

Another word for love is acceptance. When you accept your child for who they are without trying to change one ounce of them, they feel loved. Showing your child love also includes not trying to change their moods, thoughts, attitudes or beliefs.

Parents who try to "cheer their kids up" by using manipulative techniques are actually showing them the opposite of love. Manipulation is not love. Accepting your child regardless of what is going on for them *is* love. You might inspire them to feel better by lending a compassionate response but if you try to get them to feel better you are not allowing for their own emotional response.

Knowing your child's feelings will change is the best way you can accept your child without confusing their feelings with them. Your child is amazing. Show them love by believing in them. Give them all the acceptance they need so they can feel these same feelings. This doesn't mean praise them when they are making poor decisions. It means critiquing the behavior, not them.

A good parent recognizes their child is learning and instead of criticizing, they teach them.

5

Balanced Emotional Expressing

Focusing on yourself and taking care of your own emotional needs can help you be a better caregiver and bond emotionally. A child who grows up in an emotionally unsafe environment will have issues surrounding emotional security. Emotional sensitivities begin to develop after emotional inconsistencies occur. Any insecurity stems from a doubt in emotional well-being. Your emotions are like the drums in a band; life performances are better when the beat is in rhythm. There is a natural cadence in everything you do. Your emotional tempo is what harmonizes you. Sporadic emotions are nothing more than stopping the music in the middle of a song. Sometimes the halt is refreshing. Other times it interrupts everything and is the worst feeling to pick up and start to perform.

You care for yourself anytime you listen and honor to what you are feeling. When you honor your needs you stand up for yourself and communicate what you would like instead of passively aggressively getting mad if you are not getting what you need. When you listen to your feelings and trust what they are telling you, you can make better choices. Your choices are what make up the sum of your whole life. Your choices are deeply connected to what you think and feel. Any emotional experiences you are holding onto will be factored into your choices.

Life is perfect, and the way it unfolds for every individual is always perfect. There are opportunities for learning in every moment. Expose your kids to things you want them to learn by being in situations you want to be involved in. Life is really that simple with anything. Be where you want to be and go there lovingly. Each and every choice that comes from that person becomes a lesson. Each action is originated within a choice. A choice always has a consequence. When you make a choice in life notice it. What are you choosing? Your choices are the defining moments of who you are becoming. If you go in love it makes for the best journey.

There is a divine order to every choice made that sets the state for your life? When you choose love first and act with good intentions your outcome will be of that kind. Some people are very unloving no matter what. They have too many emotional wounds they have to heal before they can actually connect to another person. They use manipulation and control to get what they need. They think of themselves only. People who generate emotional conflicts haven't developed the emotional skills for coping with stress. They don't always mean to cause conflict. They my even inadvertently generate conflict by what they are emotionally suppressing. Releasing stored disappointments and old hurts generates an emotional harmony that leads to positive choices and healthy functionality.

Empower yourself by being mindful of how you express yourself. Your kids learn everything about life by the way you are handling yourself. Notice your natural actions and emotional rhythms. By now you are probably aware of what throws you off emotionally. Practice new ways of communicating. Non-violent communication, also known as NVC, has techniques to help you develop higher levels of communicating. All emotional intelligence is rooted in communication quality.

As a parent you have an added responsibility of becoming your best self while caring for the person you love the most. The entire parenting process has enormous potential for teaching you about who you are and how you can grow as a person. How you respond to life is what you teach. Everyone has a response to things that are happening. People tend to prejudge an experiences as good or bad without really emotionally weighing in everything. We don't always know where the other person is actually coming from. Your responses are a reflection of how you feel based on what you perceive is going on.

When people do not know how they feel then they are often times unaware of how they emotionally respond. Even good parents prejudged children's responses if they neglect to take the time to inquire what is going on within them. Even when you are in tune with your child it is important to take the time to ask them questions before you respond.

How you respond to your child influences their perception of who they are because perception and what we think of something, or of who we are, are two kinds of the same thing. When you respond with love then they know they are lovable. When you immediately respond with anger, they get the sense they have done something wrong. There is a possibility they were just innocently having fun and didn't mean to hurt someone. Depending on their age they may not have cognitively known any better even if you did tell them. Young minds don't register the word "don't". Make commands clear for what you do want. They actually hear what you just told them. Their minds are young and developing which means they can hold one idea to focus on. If they hear you tell them what not to do, this is what stands out in their mind. State the majority of what you say in a positive command or expectation. This approach works well for adults as well. Could you imagine going into a board meeting and only having the conductor tell you what they don't want? Specifics make a difference.

A sudden angry response might confuse them. Take the time to ask questions before discussing anything. One never really knows what is going on for another person unless the right question is asked. This means a parent has to train him or herself to ask a few questions before they explode with any type of emotional response. Expressive displays of anger rarely work to get your point across.

Explosive anger is used when someone is attacking you. A child hardly has the power to defend against a parent's rage making that display totally inappropriate. This type of emotional response usually means there are other emotional pains taking place for the parent. As one gets in touch with their full spectrum of feelings they can more easily shift their communicating.

Anger is a natural emotional filled with power to protect and transcend a problem. How you use your anger and how it is directed at people can either make or ruin relationships. All feelings are responses to what is happening. Emotion moves the feelings through expressions. Creative responses are ones that honor the feelings without being destructive. Sometimes destruction needs to occur if something is refusing to leave and is harming you. Emotional responses get altered when a person is punished for how they feel. Any action taken against someone because of how they feel is total control. Anger is a universal response for protecting the self. The key to understanding the anger is identifying what is being threatened. When you can acknowledge the fear you can disarm the anger.

The ability to respond to something is natural. It means you are alive. Angry responses occur when there is a feeling of boundaries being violated. Sorrow is a response to having lost something. Fear is a response to something unfamiliar that may cause a threat. Laughter is an emotional release to something one is observing. Laugh patterns have to do with the way a person's emotions build. No response means you are still processing. The coming together of experience and feeling hasn't happened. This can then elicit laughter with the right person. Complete unresponsiveness means that you are so closed to that particular subject, that you are disconnected from the inner and outer experience of life.

Evolved responses of love, awareness, honesty and compassion means you are able to effectively understand and even communicate your inner world to your outer reality. This is important because when one feels understood by the people in their world they feel happy. The fastest way to alleviate depression in your child is to understand them. When you respond with love and compassion your child feels heard. It soothes their emotional system which in essence is their nervous system. This allows them to be relaxed enough to communicate with their surroundings. Kids that are pensive don't feel like the world around them is safe enough to be themselves. Developing emotional responses that are loving relieves emotional stress.

A wise person discerns the difference between an unhappy feeling and bad behavior. A child that is punished for having a feeling will learn to close off to their feelings in order to make themselves more acceptable. Never punish a child for having a feeling. Recognize all behavior is an attempt to relieve a bad feeling. Acknowledge the real feelings first. Then address the behavior.

6

Creating the Framework for Good Parenting

Your child is a mirror for your life. Ultimately, children become the bi-product of the emotional expressions that take place around them. It takes a strong person to overcome their environmental influences. To a certain degree, one never really can escape their upbringing. They are forever an expression of where they come from. What one does with those influences determines who they become on their own volition.

You children become a bi-product of your emotional expressions. Overtime they take on or deny what you show them. Of course they are their own people and yet how you manage your life influences what feelings they will have to manage, but because your child is an extension of you they are going to reflect aspects of you. If you were to describe the feelings you have towards your children, you might find you would be describing your own feelings about the qualities they represent within you. The parent/child bond is powerful. Even when they are thousands of miles apart they are still connected. Parents can often times sense what is happening with their children because they are energetically connected.

The psychology of this connection can get complicated. Just because your children are your mirrors doesn't mean they will be like you. In an attempt to hold their own power, they may become your direct opposite. Separating from you like this helps them find their own power. A child who exerts strong independence and who has their own goals wants full autonomy. However, through this separation they simultaneously want to receive all the love you can give them.

Many children adapt and morph into what their parents when it earns them love and validation. Adaptation is a survival mechanism. Withholding love causes emotional afflictions. There are only certain times it is appropriate to withhold love and validation. Parents who use acceptance as a means of direction end up raising children who have a lot of emotional problems. These problems can easily pertain to people pleasing and the loss of personal self-development. When this happens a child doesn't know who they are because they are always trying to conform to someone else's expectations. How you avoid this outcome is to address the conflicts without trying to change them as a person. Modify the behavioral expectation while accepting them as their own person. In other words, reject the behavior, not them as a person. This requires a unique set of skills but it can very simply be distilled down to refraining from any and all forms of personal attack.

When any person is allowed the freedom to be who they really are, there is a peace that comes from within that has the potential to resolve any conflict. The peace that comes from a parent to child relationship has to do with how well each one accepts one another without trying to change them. You can have a deeply fulfilling relationship throughout your child's entire life just by accepting them.

The intimate dance of a parent and child always remains emotionally connected on some level. The relationship that exists between a parent and child is so powerful that it impacts every area of life, even if one isn't cognizant of how that relationship is affecting them. If there is any extreme emotional conflict between the parent or child, each individual will be affected to their core until these feelings can be heard, felt and resolved.

Kids can think they are ready for life long before they are. When thirteen-year-old is coming into themselves, they are not yet ready for life. As mature as some may act, there is still a lot that is developing inside. What independent kids are really ready for is the next step of responsibility that adds to their emotional development for handling life. Allow them to mature by adding responsibilities, but still allowing them to be kids. This seems to be a challenging concept for some parents to grasp.

Some kids get thrown into adult responsibility fast. They end up missing the natural progression of development which makes navigating adult challenges as an adult extra intimidating. The responsibility role is then acted out as an adult from the aspect of coming from a social mask. In other words, they appear confident and yet there can be a lot of childhood fears that come up. They had to assume adult-like responsibilities. Just because they handle a lot as a child doesn't necessarily make them adept at handling problems as an adult successfully. In fact, many ultra-responsible adult personalities have emotional pockets where they are extremely needy. Almost like a child would be. This is due to their own needs being denied during important stages of their life developmentally.

All problems are a result of people not getting what they need. Working through these issues comes from being aware of what was emotionally deficient and then implementing a course of self-re-parenting.

Children will always find a way through their own challenges. With every experience there will be an emotional compromise and a strength that is developed. They will make their way to their own adulthood even if you don't empower them. To support who they really are, learn to listen to their visions and support them. If you see flaws in their plans, ask them questions. You already have your heart in the right place if you are even taking the time to read this. Use inquiries that help them find the answers to their own problems. Ask them questions that help them find their own answers. Help them think and act for themselves so they can generate and amazing life when they leave home.

The development stage for leaving home is around the age of 18 or 20, unless something has gone wrong. Kids might feel afraid to leave. Or they might not know what direction they wish to be going. Or, they could have had other things happen to them. Many kids who endure abuse at home can't wait to leave and get out on their own but they can still suffer from emotional problems. Children who have spent several years from their youth being molested will have some form of emotional impediment. There will be many feelings that will affect them into adulthood. A majority of their creative and sexual power has been taken from them. No child wants to be used for someone else's satisfaction. Healing any abuse issues comes from them finding their own power that was taken.

Take care of your child by protecting them and being their best advocate. If you do these two things while giving them their freedom, you will find you can have a very enjoyable life, especially during their teen years. As a parent you have to trust the process. Your children will find the way to creating their lives on their own, even if you do or don't give them the resources.

You have about twelve years to really shape them before they are full formed. By the time they enter their teens, your role is to just be acting like the buffers for the gutter balls in the bowling alley. How they throw the ball is up to them. They don't need someone to tell them what to do or how to throw it necessarily. They are now practicing on their own and independently. Metaphorically, you might see a way for them to improve their technique, but you are there to find the best way to assert your coaching. Give too many directions and they become totally unreceptive. Don't give enough and they can make choices that are completely self-destructive.

You may even want to offer a suggestion based on what you are seeing. This feedback is quite helpful actually. However, your child is still the one playing the game. After a certain point, these are their lives. They are going to live it in a way that is of their choosing. The secret is to get the bulk of the information in before their hormones start developing.

Create a framework for your methodology for parenting. What are your personal values for living? Based on your current lifestyle and actions, what knowledge are you imparting? What course of action would you like to be imparting? Do your children think for themselves or are they always searching for someone else's love and validation? If they are, this is an indicator they haven't felt that confident. If you tell your child what to do all of the time, they will leave home conditioned not to think for themselves. Consider how you are teaching them to think for themselves?

Remember, your role is to empower and not control. Every year you are required to let go a little more. Plot the information you would like to impart and every year check in to see if you can add more. The information can pertain to health, moral values, how they can deal with difficult personalities, and the work ethic you would like them to be implementing. You have until they are about twelve until they pretend to not hear you anymore. You may even want to consider writing down all of your own anecdotes of life, for when they are ready to hear them once they are mature enough to appreciate them.

People have so much innate wisdom. All it takes is a mind that is asks questions. The more you ask questions the more you grow. Give your child a very large vocabulary to work from. Language gives people the ability to define what they see and experience. It is a tool that empowers people to handle problems. You can't solve a problem, unless you can define it. That is why language is so important. Kids who cuss typically have a very small vocabulary to work from when expressing anger or difficult emotions. When a person can match the right word with what they are feeling they connect the emotion intellectually which removes the need for behaviors that happen unconsciously.

The best way to know your child is feeling safe and secure is to resolve all emotions as they come up. The more peaceful and happy you are the better off they are. If you have stagnation in your emotional system it's because you've probably had relationships in which you had to shut down. When you are shut down emotionally you close off to intimacy.

Develop a language for feelings in your household. At first it may get old hearing how everybody feels but it's the fastest way towards connection. A good parent is there to mirror back to their child how they feel, not alter their emotions. When you raise a kid with a high level of emotional awareness, you raise an empowered kid. You can only facilitate emotional intelligence if you yourself are aware of your own feelings. You help all people when you validate their feelings. Notice all behaviors and see them as how someone is emotionally responding to life. When you understand that a person's expressions are the result of what they are feeling, there is no need to get upset, offended, or take things personally. When you validate a person's feelings by acknowledging what they are either saying or showing, it typically diffuses conflict unless they are so guarded all they want to do is bully.

As a parent it is important to remember during times of conflict that your child is their own person. They won't have the capacity to appreciate you or understand you until he or she becomes a fuller person. You are caring for them until they are able to develop into themselves. Your job is to see that all of your children are fully developed on the inside, as much as they can be, before they leave home. An indicator of maturity is when they appreciate you for all you have done. This doesn't always mean they will appreciate all you have done for them as they are waving goodbye on their journey. It may take them awhile to have enough life experiences to fully appreciate and value you. When they do, you know your role as parent is through. This emotional connection is powerful. The end always comes and a new beginning shows signs of emerging. The more comfortable you are during these transitions the more you will enjoy the process of parenting.

Emotion is the movement of feelings. Children with harmonious rhythms and routines feel good inside.

7

Making Life Perfect

Your life does not have to be perfect to raise a happy child. You might have a lot of missing pieces. You may struggle with your relationships, responsibilities and caring for yourself and everyone else, but if you remain connected to your own true feelings, you can go through anything. When you are in your power you are aware of how you are responding. Your emotional responses to life are what give your life meaning. You may have everything in your world crashing down but if you remain connected to your own true feelings you can go through anything. No one is responsible for anyone's happiness. You are not responsible for your child's happiness. You are responsible for their wellbeing, while they are developing.

You are your child's leader. Empower yourself so that you are responding to life and not just unconsciously reacting. When you act with love in all situations you have the capacity to see life from all angels. Blaming others is driven by the inability to ask for help. Anyone whose actions communicate anything less than love is not seeing the full picture.

Find healthier outlets for stress other than yelling, hitting, fighting or substances such as food, alcohol or relationships. These are all coping skills that lead to more stress. Find a way to empower yourself so that you can be the best. You can have the best life when you learn to feel what you really feel. Take responsibility and make choices that empower yourself.

Stress and emotional obstacles are a part of life. People who get used to it are more well-adjusted and have better inner tools. It is incredibly important for parents to seek help for their own emotional problems, for the sakes of their children. Anytime a parent has to contend with a trauma it affects the entire family system. In fact, anytime anyone in the family has to contend with a trauma it affects the entire family system.

Eventually, if the parent or other family member doesn't get help it affects everyone. People know this, yet they don't seek help, when they are in crisis. This is because we don't know who to trust or turn to for help. It takes a lot of money to seek quality help to be happy. This book will help you. The more peaceful you can be as parent by healing emotional wounds the more your children can grow up to be who they were meant to be happy and fulfilled. There is no sense drawing out the emotional pain one more day.

Tough love is a technique used to reform bad behavior but most people confuse the true meaning of tough love. Parents who attempt to control their children with love can create many problems that backfire later on. Tough love is disapproving of the behavior, not the individual themselves.

Children must be allowed their full range of emotions. If they are punished for how they feel or the mood they are in then they are not being given the right to feel their full range of emotion.

If a child suppresses emotion it will only come up later on in some form of destructive behaviors. A child may hold onto the emotion from suppression that causes health problems, or conflicts. The behaviors of addictions and/or self-mutilation are all indicators feelings have built up. Frustration can be expressed in any way such as violence or stealing. To decode certain behaviors it is always important to look to the underlying feelings that could possibly be driving the behavior. You can reject the behavior but not who your child is as an individual.

Any problem can be solved when approached with love. Most interpersonal problems are generated from a lack of love. If two or more people know how to emotionally organize the content of the problem they can begin to find the solutions which are always based in love.

There must always be a baseline of love in a home. If a home doesn't have love then it will only produce waves of destruction. A family can heal from any problem when there is emotional honesty and a willingness to change.

Some resentment run so deep that certain family members are unbending. All you can do is accept the other person's feelings. The only way to know how to handle your feelings is to trust them. Always act with love. This doesn't mean allow them to treat you badly.

Love isn't tolerating someone's abuse. Love is allowing everyone to be who they are while you be your best you. Accept the situation for what it is. Do your best to avoid further conflicts. In time the other person may come around, or not.

Every relationship is up to the people involved. Anything can be healed with truth and love. The same is true for you and your child. No matter where you've been or what road you are on, you can heal and so can your child. There are many great therapists with unique techniques to help you, your family and your child heal from anything that has gone on.

A good parent or parents will have a healthy command over their family system so that it can serve each member individually while sustaining its system.

8

Behavior as Emotional Language

Babies are completely emotionally in tune with their feelings. They express what they need through the expression of their feelings. Their cognitive capacity for mental intelligence is preparing for information. They have no information as to how to act or respond. According to some specialists they have their two basic fears of falling and loud noises. All of the other fears are apparently derived from all other experiences.

In the beginning their development requires physical comfort, nutrition and sleep. Their minds have no limiting beliefs that stop them from responding completely and uninhibitedly to their needs. They cry when they are hungry. They fuss when they are uncomfortable. They are discontent when the energy around them isn't peaceful. They are preparing for life and require constant attention.

Tending to your baby's every need in the first two years will have established a very solid sense of security deep within their psyche. They need this trust to develop and grow. Parents who "train" their kids early will help them for the rest of their life.

Babies are completely helpless. They are dependent on their parent's emotional need to give to them. If they don't get what they need they won't survive. If you are not in tune with your child's emotional needs they will feel empty and removed from the relationship. If this emotional lack of emotional connection is sustained long enough they won't develop adequately.

Some parents find their children's emotional cues annoying. They might even scold them for expressing. This trains children, early on, to shut down to what they are feeling. Without the ability to feel or express feelings they get bottled up, which leads to all sorts of problems mentally, emotionally and physically.

Everybody needs an emotional outlet. Without a way of expressing feelings inside, the self gets lost and needs go unmet. A child will shut down emotionally just to cope. Parents who respond aggressively to a child who is just simply emotionally expressing usually don't like the behavior their kid is triggering inside. They think if they can get their kid to be quiet, then, they will be able to go back to feeling good too. This is sometimes the case but not with deep emotional feelings that are coming through.

Contending with emotions can be annoying. When you don't know what your children want, and they are misbehaving, it provokes other feelings, within yourself, to contend with, such as helplessness, frustration, and fear. Feelings are the energy that leads to the survival of the real self. Suppressing people's real feelings gives power to the person who can turn them off. If a person can cause you to shut down to your feeling they can control you. This is what parents do to their kids and it is unhealthy. It leads to unhappy lives and poor choices. For a child to be successful they have to be connected to their feelings.

Kids use behavior when they don't have the words inside. A child should never be punished for how they feel. This doesn't mean they should violate other people with their feelings. Violations are only a sign of aggressive behavior. If they had a constructive outlet for the anger they wouldn't have to take it out on other people. All behaviors make sense when one can get to the true feelings. That's the problem. A lot of people don't know what they are feeling and end up acting unconsciously which ends up influencing a situation negatively.

Each parent gets to define how far the expressions will be able to be expressed before they shut the child down for being what some may term annoying. Emotional expressions in the form of behavior are different from the feelings underlying the behavior. A child should never be punished for their feelings.

The best method is to teach through explanation, which takes a lot of time, but it is well worth it. This doesn't mean long lectures but rather four to ten sentences. The time gets factored in every time you have to do it. They have growing minds and each day is a new experience.

Most children after the age of 4-5 should have light consequences for actions they have taken that are out of line. Any punishment must be seriously considered before acted upon because it is incredibly traumatizing to a child. To endure a punishment for what they don't even have cognitive skills for does nothing in the long run except for teach them the behavior you may or may not want.

Kids before the age of 5 are usually just expressing what others do or has been done to them. They don't have the cognitive ability to make a strict punishment effective. Before the age of about 5, what they really need is communication and explanation. They need love and information. All they want to do is please at this age anyway, unless they have already been tormented. Then they are just acting out to find relief for their uncomfortable feelings.

A young child is already attempting to learn right from wrong. The mental observations that take place within their mind are part of their survival mechanisms. What they observe within their social structure is taken in as information that creates "yes" or "no" like commands for what is or isn't acceptable. They intuitively develop this ability to know what is or isn't acceptable for their acceptance. They may close off to important aspects that serve for their survival if harsh punishments are incurred. Strict forms of punishment can cause them to close down to other natural expressions that can be quite adorable. A super controlled kid might be polite but they don't act natural. There is a lot of emotion that can brew beneath the social niceties formed through strict parenting.

You can see the vacancy in a kid's eyes who has been abused while being reprimanded. They are disconnected from themselves. They don't have their full capacity for feeling. They have had to shut down emotionally. This closing off to the world can easily lead to emotional difficulties such as poverty and difficulties with intimacy. Recovering the lost self means healing all of the feelings that one has separated from in order to survive emotionally.

Denials preserve survival at certain stages. When a person develops enough psychological space that they can no longer hold onto the denials, enormous pain begins and as a result they must shed what they were once holding. Psychological pain is a sign there is a belief that needs changing. Remaining connected to the feelings is how the real self can come out of hiding. People avoid their real feelings because they literally feel like they are dying. Adults eventually "die" from not feeling their true feelings. Children "die" from having absolutely no one there to physically, mentally and emotionally comfort them.

Emotion that can't go anywhere and has no words to match up with cognitive meaning is raw energy that has the potential to destroy people, families and individual dreams. The denial preserves the self that finds the emotion too overwhelming. All people require love, acceptance and validation.

Living in psychological lies produces an emotional state that is incredibly painful. In fact, some people die prematurely because there is no outlet for the pain. Teens commit suicide because of the longstanding emotional pain they can't identify. They become trapped in behaviors that are not resourceful, because they can't find the relief, inside. When any person, adult or child, can cognitively connect to the true feelings inside by matching what they feel to a verbal articulation, they bridge understanding with thought and feeling. This bridge brings relief to any emotion they are feeling. If a person can state how they feel and be heard, it relieves all the pain that has been stored along with the feelings. This is your job as an emotionally intelligent parent; listen and validate your child. This doesn't mean condone the behavior. It means allow yourself to receive what they are really feeling.

A child who never had their needs met has to learn as an adult how to function in society. The standard or irregular emotional response that comes from the parents and people around them shapes them emotionally. Moodiness affects kids dramatically. As they grow older their intellect begins to take shape. They have learned through their environment what emotions they can and can't express. This behavioral reinforcement that occurs influences who they are and what they reveal to the rest of the world. The emotional feedback they get will be used as information when they go out into the world as they get older. If they are emotionally healthy they will be able to get their needs met. If they are beaten down inside emotionally they will always struggle on some level until they can get help.

A good feeling means a need is being met. A bad feeling is an indicator a need is not being met.

9

Emotional Wellness as a Parent

All people need emotional wellness to feel happy. The problem many parents seem to forget is that having a baby is only the start of the emotional marathon you will be running to care for them. Most people can't even run a 26 mile marathon with their own physical body let alone raise a child for nearly 26 years until they are fully healthy and ready.

Mother Nature gives you a series of ages and stages that allow you to condition yourself as you go. There are intermittent periods of parenthood that force us to grow. You might even notice how you use up so much energy in the beginning throwing elaborate baby showers or extravagant birthday parties. Some parents have burnt themselves out by the time the child is 8 leaving little to no energy left for the other stages. A parent can easily become complacent and stop responding to the children's needs because they are already so tired from just surviving.

Being a parent is not about being the world's best. It is about raising your child so they can grow up and function in society. They need to express themselves creatively and receive money for it. They need to have loving relationships. And they need to make the money they need to live. And with the extra energy that is left, then pursue a few dreams along the way.

Like any human being, children want to know they are wanted and valuable. How you treat them affects how they use their creative power. Will they use their creative energy for good? Will they have love in their heart? Or, will they use creative energy in a destructive way because they are tormented inside?

Children must first be given love, before they can act with love. When they are loved they will use their creative energy for good. When they are tormented from all the dysfunction and emotional pain they will struggle and their creative energy can become destructive? When children feel loved and acknowledged they will be less apt to travel down roads of destruction.

No child ever grows up and says, "I want to be a murderer," "I want to be a thief," or "I want to be single for the rest of my life." They don't ever think they're going to hate their parents or live on the street. They are just doing the things that they were unconsciously trained to do.

Emotions are natural responses. They are nothing more than energy movements from perceptions of things coming out at us. Troubled kids have to cope with challenging situations. The lack of emotional awareness exacerbates these problems. All human beings have their own particular mental and emotional program that trains them to operate in a certain way. These messages we receive when we are young can become mental programs for personal operation. People do things because of the way there inner lives have been shaped. Rising above these challenges takes a huge amount of emotional awareness.

There are a lot of situations that come up in one's life that won't be understood or anticipate. One cannot predict or completely foresee what will happen but there are certain behaviors that will influence one's direction.

Raising a healthy child who functions well in the world begins with a fully-functioning emotion. The greater a person's mental and emotional awareness, the happier they are no matter what age they are. The more intelligent and emotionally aware you are the more capacity you have for solving problems as they arise.

As a mature adult, you eventually begin to see how to be in the role of "parent" in your life. You are playing many roles such as a coach, caretaker, educator. Part of the parental journey is about finding out what you had to overcome in order to get to what you know. Anyone who parents actively and with intentionality should have a certificate of recognition for something amazing. You are as a parent are the full realization of what has taken place over history. This evaluation usual takes place after one's children are grown. However, if you review your performance regularly, you may find many reasons to praise yourself parentally.

It can be helpful to think of your parenting process much like the pregnancy experience. You are given nine months to grow a healthy, full term baby. You have about 18 years to get in everything they need to know before that baby enters the world as an adult. If you stay ahead of the game and evolve mentally and emotionally as a parent you will have no problem seeing your way to the finish line having raised a perfectly healthy, well-adjusted and balanced individual. This doesn't always mean everything will be easy. However, if you stay on top of things you can handle anything that is happening.

There will be growing pains along the way and the empty nest syndrome, which is the psychological equivalency of labor. Just like when you anticipated the arrival of your baby, you are anticipating the arrival of who they are as an adult. You get to enjoy their childlike gestational periods each and every day until they leave home. Just like the hormonal changes that took place during pregnancy, your hormones will change during the duration of rearing your child. These will influence your thinking and states of being. You are now older and with everything that took place you may wonder where did the time go?

Mother Nature operates in such divine perfection. There is an evolutionary process for flow. The best thing anyone can do is their best while, at the same time, lightening up. There are no gold medals at the end of this marathon. The work you put into it is for yourself and others. You may even find your family is totally ungrateful for all you have sacrificed. No one really understands what a parent forfeits in devotion to their children. The reward you do get is all the wisdom you harvest inside. Parenting teaches you how much capacity you have inside to thrive. You are amazingly resilient. You have the power inside to create a life exactly how you want. The effort that comes from loving so much unlocks this enormous potential inside. You have become stronger than any Olympic athlete because you stuck through an enormously demanding process and never gave up. When you succeed at sitting back and enjoy the daily interactions you eventually reach the finish line feeling satisfied.

Just because you are a parent does not mean you need to take on the responsibilities of the entire world. People abdicate their responsibilities and gladly place them onto others. Other parents need to do their jobs too. You stay focused on your family and allow other people to do what they need to do. The same is true within your own family.

Individuals are responsible for creating their own lives. The job is not entirely up to you. Present the opportunities but the children choose. As you stay focused on what you are doing everything in your life organizes to align with what you are doing. When you focus on what others are doing, your bottom falls out. Make every day fun. Learn from the experience and open your heart to love.

Becoming a parent is one of the most significant of the experiences that evolve who you are. You are now caring for another individual. You have no idea what this will do to your soul. For many people this is good. For emotional caretaking perfectionists it will be exhausting. Your mind, as a parent, is probably a lot different than it was when you were single. If parenting doesn't change you, it might be because enough time, focus, effort or mindfulness put into it. And yet the after affects lack of commitment will have enough of an impact that will still have the power to change you. The mind altering affect parenting has on the brain is really no different from the pregnancy brain that sets in, once you are pregnant. You are now hardwired to protect, preserve and care for this child. At a fundamental level you are now making decisions that you once would not have made.

If you are the type of person who wants to please people, you are most likely now managing your life for your child's wellbeing instead of your own. If you have codependency issues you may forget to include yourself into the decisionmaking. This can generate a heavy burden if circumstances mean support is sparse and the workload is left all to you. All of these can be managed though by being the most balanced you. Your emotional intent for protecting both you and the wellbeing for your offspring has to do with the unconscious emotional content you are holding onto. Your emotional intention toward your child's protection has a lot to do with what you have lived through.

You will parent from the mindset from that you survived your own emotional challenges from childhood. The only flaw in this concept is, most likely, your children will have a completely different set of circumstances than you did. What this means is you might be overlooking what your children need from you and protecting them from them from a phantom that isn't even there. You might actually not even see what they need protection from if you are not seeing beyond your own fears.

The only way to detect valid threats is to trust each and every gut feeling you get. Pay attention. Listen to your stomach. Listen to your intuitive flashes. Listen to your children and their intuitive senses. On some level you know exactly what is happening. If your mind doesn't have a clue, your body does. All you have to do is access your body's intuition. You have to be emotionally awake to be effective at giving your kids what they need. When you trust your gut, you have the potential of a thriving family.

Managing emotion generated from parenting is a lot like managing the hormones that were created in the woman's body during pregnancy. There are real psychological pressures that come from caring for somebody. These pressures are real. They take a strong emotional constitution to work through. You have to stay aligned to your inner truth. You have to align the visions of your own with your families. You have to follow what you feel is intuitively correct to do. And you have to be happy. When you are happy you will naturally be a more responsive parent.

Children are naturally happy and abundant with potential. You could pretty much do everything with love in your heart and have you child turn out to be their own kind of perfect. Kids are amazing, and so are you as a parent. When you manage your feelings back to a state of happiness you create a loving opportunity for them to learn and grow into the people you envision them becoming. You deserve so much recognition for caring so much about them.

People who avoid conflict do whatever they can to stay out of a confrontation of any kind. They may acquiesce to others demands so they can avoid conflict. Knowing how to face conflict in a powerful way is probably one of the best skills one can ever learn as a parent. Your family's wellbeing has to do with how you protect it. There is a fine balance; protect it too much and you close off to opportunities. Don't protect it enough and you expose members to certain toxicities. Standing up for your kids requires the ability to confront conflict head on in a way that stops the problem. Sometimes your job as a parent is to act like a killer T-cell and destroy what invader has just come at it. What this looks like will vary from person to person. This is the same knowledge you need for life. If you can develop this understanding before pregnancy, your life will be even better.

A people pleaser will avoid standing up in situations that are quite necessary to do so. People who avoid conflict end up losing control over their lives. Unless they learn to stand up for themselves they won't be able to do what they want to. Rejecting a child when they don't do what you want them to do is one of the best way to raise a people pleaser. They might make learn to make you happy but as adults they are miserable.

As a parent you have to become good at managing your emotional responses. Communication skills are what you are continuously developing, as a parent. Being a responsible adult comes from knowing how to minimize conflict without compromising yourself. You can have all the feelings you have, but you have to be mindful of you express them, otherwise you end up adversely affecting your children. The pressures that come from caring for another person create emotions that can't be allowed to get out of control. Managing those emotions constitutes being in your power.

Extreme hypervigilance, in the form of an extreme need to protect, often springs from an unconscious need to fulfill what was lacking in one's own childhood. People who felt a constant threat, as children, will most likely feel a constant need to protect their own children. As a parent you geared for the survival and nurturing of this baby. The overtones expressed in your personality have to do with your own history. If they are working effectively, you will want to keep them. If something isn't working with your parenting, because it's being reflected back to you, in your childrens' behavior, there may be something to find out about yourself, by looking deeper.

The more difficult time you had emotionally when you were younger, the more emotional content you will most likely have to work through as a parent. The more love you feel as you transition into this new phase of your life the better off you are as a parent. Each stage of parenting requires a huge amount of emotional energy and love. If you are already a parent who is depleted of love it will be more challenging for you to give love because you are attempting to give what you don't have. A parent's role is to give adequate warmth and responsiveness to each child. Get ahead of any problem by creating as much balance and functionality in your own life so that your family can thrive.

Everything you give or don't give affects your child. Everything they receive or don't receive shapes them. Whatever you wish for your child and can't give them, shapes who they are just as much as what you *do* give them.

It is very stressful not to have the resources to adequately pull through and do the job you really want to do. The deficient resources can be anything from love, trust, money, emotional support or the warmth of the community you belong to. Whatever you wish for your child is often times what wasn't supplied for you. Your mindset as a parent is usually a mirror for the inner work you have to do. Your children are your mirrors. They get to reflect back what is going on for you.

A lot of parents can be so out of touch with their own feelings that they project their feelings onto their kids. Projection takes place when you see them as anything less than their own person. When you love your child in every single moment with the fullest love and compassion then you know you are enlightened. In the meantime you can operate from guidelines.

A parent who believes they are inadequate before they have children may find their feelings of inadequacy are magnified times ten once they are assuming responsibility for another human. Your child is your most beautiful creation. You want to give them everything you are so they can grow to become who they are meant to be.

10

Remaining Emotionally Connected

There are many people who will impact your children's development, but the most impactful role is the one of the parent. You as the parent have the final say in everything they choose. You are either with them offering them support, protection and guidance or you are off doing your own thing.

Your level of mental and emotional presence will be what influences their emotional lives. The more you engage with them and participate in what is happening in their own life, the more connected and loving you are to them. The more engaged you are the more significant you become to them. If you pay no attention to them they're not going to consider you a valuable emotional asset. They will close off to you because they will sense you are not there for them.

When a child closes off to their parent it means you have lost them. When you've lost them there is no telling what will happen to them. You must keep a good connection with your child if you are to effectively parent them.

You can tell when a connection has been lost when you're no longer getting feedback from them. If you are stressed out and dealing with your own problems then you will pay less attention to them. After a while this takes a toll on the relationship. You can be around your child all of the time, yet never connect to them. Connection means you're looking at them. You are interacting with what's happening inside of them. It means you are seeing them for who they really are and not just talking to them. Real connections come from a genuine exchange. You are sharing with them who you are and they are doing the same. You have no connection with your child when they give you nothing.

You can at any time begin to change the way you connect to your child by changing the way you interact with them. A child will naturally connect to the parent that protects and loves. With the loss of stay-at-home moms, women are providing less and less emotional protection to their child.

The more a woman attempts to masculinize herself in an attempt to feel power, she ends up losing her power as a woman. A father plays the role of physically protecting his family by providing for them financially and physically guarding. When a man cheats it is extra painful because he has just exposed the family to a huge vulnerability. A man who is not a provider and cheats will still have an impact but not as much because the threat isn't the same. He is already neglecting his duties so it is now just one more thing added.

There are many relational problems that happen in a family that affect the way the kids connect to the parents. A woman who cheats weakens her family. She is trying to get her needs met outside of the family through infidelity. This breaks down the family unit even if the family functioning is already unhealthy. It also can emasculate a man's power to protect and provide.

A man can easily perceive himself as having not provided enough so she strays. A man who is dedicated to providing will be impacted the most. If a woman has no capacity to see or appreciate him for what a good provider has been, she will minimize his emotions and just move on. This is a doubly painful emotional response to a man who has just provided for the family he is working for. A man who thinks he is not enough will continue to stay, in attempt to prove himself again.

Affairs are incredibly painful for children even if they never know about them. The wounds they inflict in the other parent impacts the parent's parental role not to mention their own personal well-being and health.

There are many different relational dynamics that take place that affect people emotionally. The children's ability to connect to others is a learned skill based on how well the parents connect to each other and how the child connects to each parent. Each parent's daily emotions will affect how they connect with their child on a regular basis. A child needs both parents to be whole and intact in order for him to develop with full confidence. Any compromising situation that impacts the parent will impact the child.

A broken family dynamic impacts everyone. Broken means pieces are missing and the family system is compromised. The structure bears and extra burden. When kids must manage themselves, instead of just being happy kids who manage themselves they can't partake in the normal kid stuff of growing up. When parent's divorces there has to be emotional work so the kids can adjust to a new dynamic. They are now developing their own individual relationship with each parent that is separate from the family unit.

You as the parent are responsible for caring for your child for a very long time. You are also responsible for caring for yourself. You have to do the things that bring yourself joy. If being involved with a destructive spouse then divorce becomes the option. As a parent you have a choice to make in how you maneuver through your life. You also have a choice as to how well you interact with your child. You can either be proactive or let your child stand alone and learn to fend for themselves.

If you have any stored feelings that you faced it will create emotional responses that affect them in very specific ways. Connect to what you feel so your kids can have their own feelings.

11

The Seven Stages of Preparing Your Child for the Future

Knowing how to emotionally prepare your children for their future comes from observing who they are and who they are not. Knowing who they are at their deepest level allows you to support their true individuality. When you know who they are you can be more effective at giving them what they really need.

Parents can make the mistake of trying to give their kids what they really don't need. Without thinking, first, they may offer unsolicited or fear-based thinking. If you tell your children about every problem they might encounter, you might scare them. If you over teach them they may not have their own ability to come up with their own solutions.

You never know fully what your children might need. After a certain age their lives become of their own choosing. Fighting against resistance never works. You as the parent have to inspire their own thinking. There are signs that you could guess at, but ultimately, each of their lives is a mystery unfolding, just as yours is.

There are seven stages of parenting to actively involve yourself in as a parent. Each stage is equally important for laying the groundwork for adulthood. The first stage is pregnancy through infancy. This is the stage where you take care of your baby's nutritional nourishment, love and comfort. You are tending to the baby's most basic of needs to give them a chance to grow healthily in every way.

The second stage of parenting occurs when babies are toddlers, ready to start exploring the world around them. They need the freedom to explore while being monitored. The second stage is when the ego begins to develop. Everything they are told about themselves goes into their minds and begins to form a self-concept. In the second stage, it's incredibly important to be positive about your attitude towards your child because your opinion contributes to their overall ideas and opinions about themselves. Kids can sense other people's opinions towards them. This will influence how their psyche develops about who they are as well as several other mental functions.

Whatever you say to your child during this stage sets the foundation for their entire sense of self. Refrain from any negative dialogue that may adversely affect their self-concept. Absolutely eliminate any and all negative criticisms or judgments about who they are, what they choose and how they are doing something. You can offer constructive suggestions, but once again, approach all critique with inquiry. If their behavior bothers or confuses you, ask them why they do that particular thing and you may find an entire world opening up about their psyche. Just refrain from directing any criticism at them during this second stage. The thoughts formed by other people's suggestions or opinions will form their mental programs that will influence them for the rest of their life.

The third stage of life comes when your children are getting ready to go to school. They are getting ready to leave home and be without you. They're going out into the world and forming relationships of their own. What children need most during this time is a parent who supports them. Kids don't know how to make friends. They need to learn social skills. They need a coach who's there, and available, at almost every moment if a conflict arises.

Kids do not have the defenses to be able to handle bullying, peer pressure or negative influences at this stage. They need to be protected while they form their own relationships. A parent who is too overbearing is a parent who is too controlling. Children want to make their own choices, but need someone there monitoring.

The fourth stage of parenting occurs right before puberty. This is when children are developing their developing their creative autonomy. They are starting to dress the way they want to. They are doing their hair the way they want to. They are associating with the world around them in a way that is unique to them. What kids need at this stage is their creative freedom. They need to be exposed to things they find fun—as many as possible.

This stage will influence what they do as adults. If kids at this age do not have good relationships it will influence their self-concept. They will feel alone and isolated. At this stage, good parents give their children access to everything they will need to form their own lives. They need good health care. They need good hygiene habits. They need access to resources that help them be who they are like clothes that express who they really are, a bedroom that is decorated the way they like or access to people and activities they enjoy. Children need creative outlets. They need activities that stimulate them. They also need the feeling that life supports them. This sense of support cannot come from one parent alone. This support comes from a loving community that envelops them. Church, school, extracurricular activities are all ways to give children a sense of community, during the fourth stage of parenting.

The fifth stage of parenting comes when your child is maturing and going through puberty. At this point in a child's life, the parent is no longer as important as they were before. They will now get their needs met by looking for love and attention from the opposite sex. They will now look to external factors to get their needs met. Any deficiencies in their upbringing are going to show up in what they are seeking. The more you as a parent can supply these needs by giving your child access to environments from which they can actively seek out what they need on their own, the more they can thrive in this stage. Restricting them in this stage is detrimental because they need these social interactions from positive outside influences to develop their independent social skills for life.

During this fifth stage your child is learning about everything they possibly can about life. This is a very important stage preparing them for real life. The common mistake that parents make is protecting their children too much, so they miss out on opportunities from which they otherwise might have learned a lot. The best thing a parent can do in this fifth stage of parenting is to be there for their child, whenever a question comes up. Remember, if you want your children to be ready for life, you want to give them the opportunity to go through all the necessary stages of exploring life on their own. What happens in the fifth stage of parenting determines whether or not your children will be ready to leave home. Will they get their lessons or will you control?

The sixth stage of parenting is when your child has earned themselves the rights to their freedom in your home. This means they are responsible. They come home on time. They're holding down a steady job perhaps. They treat people with respect. They are showing good communication skills, and by doing so, they have earned extra privileges. They have earned your trust. There is still a possibility that they may mess up, but for the most part they seem to have what they're doing in order.

The sixth stage is also when your children need to be rewarded and recognized for all that they are doing right. You need to give them as much verbal praise as you can when they do something good. This is the stage where you build their confidence. This is also the stage when they are preparing realistically to leave home. Everything you do now is helping them learn the life skills they need to be able to leave home. The sixth stage of parenting can feel as though your job is finished. However, the stage that comes next is the most important.

The seventh stage of parenting is when your child finally leaves home. You think you're done but you're not. What happens to children, when they leave home, is going to set the precedent for their young adulthood, just as their infancy set the tone for their entire development. What happens when your kids leave home is what will happen in their young adulthood. If there is anything tragic that happens to them you must love them through it. You can't rescue them and bring them home unless it's incredibly tragic. Hopefully you have given your young adult children the skills they need to start directing their lives the way they want them to be.

If you try to control in this stage of their lives it will be a disaster. You have already played out a significant part of your role. Your role now is having to let them go. You have hopefully had some practice since this is what you have been doing since they were a preteen. This is different though. When you let them go make sure that your attitude is happy and joyous. Your attitude about them makes all the difference in the world. The more your child knows you have genuine faith in them and their capabilities the more they will succeed.

A family that prevents an adult child from leaving home has codependency issues. Criticizing your children isn't going to help you. Look at how you are holding onto them. Is there something you know you did that affected them which causes you to still hold onto them? Adult child is ultimately responsible for their own healing. However, a family that doesn't allow each person to be themselves is operating through emotional enmeshment.

When a person can't decipher their own true feelings, they are not operating as an empowered human being. A person can't feel the truth of who they are if they are still stuck in a dysfunctional family system. The person in charge of the family dictates to them whether or not what they feel is accurate. Once children are allowed to break free they have found their power and they are ready to choose the lives they are meant to be living.

Teach your children how to stand in their power by giving them their power in increments. At every stage in their lives there will be an opportunity to give or withhold their power. Within each one of these stages there is a lesson or a task they have to learn in order to get to where they need to be to earn this power. This power is not earned by making a parent happy. This power is earned by being emotionally ready. Your adult child may never be who you want them to be but you have to let them go. You know they are ready when they can live life on their own.

Just like building a home, raising a mentally and emotionally healthy child into adulthood is a process. Each stage lays down its own equally-important foundation, to help them flourish throughout the process of leaving home.

12

Being In Command of Your Family

As a parent, you most likely have many dreams for yourself and your family. You have all the capacity to accomplish those dreams when you use your emotional power in a loving way. A good family has never been built on control and power. A good family is built on love, nurturance and understanding each individual.

When parents get upset it is because they are judging something as wrong or bad. Parents are not perfect. Many are still adult children themselves. A parent who understands the full situation would never diminish the value of child in a time of stress or catastrophe. Parental responses are as innocent as the children they are raising. Everyone makes mistakes. It is up to you to learn from yours and self-correct.

When you parent from an open heart your parenting skills will be a huge success. You do not need to override your own instincts. You know what to do when you are quiet enough to hear the guidance.

Children can easily become a target for parents' pent-up stress. The complexities of responsibility are a lot for a parent to manage emotionally. If you as a parent are not coping well with life you will become just as defensive as a child. A parent can isolate, become moody or become addicted to substances in an attempt to relieve stress. The mind can only handle so much psychological stress before it breaks.

Parents who beat their children and say they're doing it out of love are really they are doing it out of love are really just taking their anger out on another person. True love never looks like a beating, verbal beating or withholding. Parents need to diligently manage their own emotions so they don't take their feelings out on others. Parents have to learn to support themselves while managing some difficult relationships.

When you are happy you are in your power. When you are in your power you are in command of your family. Command is a different type of power than control. Many parents can easily abuse through their sense of authority. Abuse in any form takes the personal rights away from the individual.

There are always five main rights that uphold respect. They are the right to feel the way you feel; the right to think the way you think; the right to say how you feel about something in a way that is mutually honoring; the right to have control over your body; and the right to choose what you want to be choosing.

You have a unique path you are on and your children are a part of it. Enjoy them. Be with them. Let go of the fear of doing it "wrong" Be happy to spend time with them no matter what the extenuating circumstances are.

The quality of your relationship with them is the sum of all the memorable moments you have taken the time to have with them.

A healthy family always has leaders who are in their power. Empowered parents are those who make their children respect their authority. When you treat kids in a lovable and respectful way they remember this and respond similarly. A parent who feels disrespected should first evaluate his or her way of responding to the children. Often there is something coming up in the parents communication style that is causing friction. Miscommunication can happen in any relationship. Honest, clear communication is what prevents and resolves conflict.

Being in command creates harmonious order. When you are in command you are leading your family to something better. You inspire your family to be their best. When you exert control, you are taking power away from other individuals. Real leadership is possible only when there are healthy and consistent boundaries that keep the family system running smoothly. Good leadership inspires the individual to be organized because they want to be. They see the benefits and are rewarded consistently. The individuals each take pride over their own lives while feeling a strong sense of belonging. They feel needed and important so they easily contribute to the overall family function in a positive way. They don't lose themselves in taking care of someone else's problems, because they have been well taught to operate interdependently which means they can acknowledge someone's experience without having to give up who they are to accommodate them.

A dysfunctional family is enmeshed. The emotional system for operation is not self-serving. Enmeshment means efforts are motivated by avoiding pain or rejection. They are codependent and inconsistently rewarding. A person can make a family work by being controlling however this doesn't make them in command. It makes them a dictator. A dictator may have control but no one is happy. The family members act like servants and can't wait to leave. Or else they are so beaten down they don't know how to function without someone acting as their authority. They end up staying with the family because they can't seem to muster the personal power to leave. They were never allowed to have the freedom they needed to be fully functioning.

Kids who are out of control usually have no one leading them. A loving leader is what an out of control family needs in order for an out of control family to get back in control as long as the boundaries they set are all consistent and healthy. Parents can lose control over their lives. Children can go astray. A family can become preoccupied with all of the stresses of life and it takes a good leader to help everyone find their way.

A parent who can understand the fine line between giving too much freedom and having too much power and control can find the balance and know where they're coming from. A parent who is too eager to control has issues of fear that must be worked through. A parent who gives away too much freedom does not understand a child's emotional and mental development. Kids have to have structure to some extent. A very loving parent might not realize what they are doing when they maintain a life that is inconsistent. It can be helpful for these personality types to use social structures that help instill routine such as martial arts classes or other means.

There are many good parents who are inconsistent in their routine. This is challenging for some personalities. Most experts say all kids need a good routine, however, some routines are too rigid and don't allow for any enjoyment or spontaneity. Routine is important. How you choose to run your family will be up to your personality.

The key to success in parenting is maintaining consistent boundaries. Even if the routine changes, emotional boundaries need to remain consistent for healthy emotional development. Inconsistent behavior just adds to a child's emotional responsibilities. Monitoring inconsistencies in the environment can become a full time job for a child who has to answer to such authority. Even if your schedule is sporadic, if you can maintain emotional consistency you build a solid inner foundation. Set healthy emotional boundaries by remaining consistent.

Every person needs self-discipline. A happy life comes from this type of empowerment. If there is no self-discipline people can't get to their goals. The mistake some parents make is controlling their children as if to impose their own disciplinary rules on them. This is not helpful. Children do not learn positive self-discipline by being heavily controlled. They build resentment and later on in life have to work through issues of control.

The secondary problem is that parents are now raising kids without any control. Having balanced leadership that's interdependent with freedom can still allow a child to choose certain things but there's also a natural consequence for choices. Life is filled with natural consequences. If there is no consequence at home the kids are in for a rude awakening when they leave home. There are consequences for everything choice we make in life. When you reinforce consequences that are in alignment with natural consequences, you actually help your child adapt to real-life occurrences.

Disciplinary procedures must be performed strategically and consistently. It cannot be in the form of abuse or demeaning rigidity. Abuse just makes the emotions do all sorts of things that are destructive. The problem that can arise in a dictatorship are the secondary emotions that come from cruel aggression. It can foster passive aggressive tendencies along with people pleasing passiveness. A parent or any person who tries to take over the faculties of someone else by telling them what they should think, feel or choose is actually in violation of their child's free will. This is a form of abuse towards another individual. Your child will either choose to do what they need to do or they won't. You cannot control what they can choose. The only thing you can control is the consequence.

It can be confusing for a child when the parents act as controlling dictators but give out love and acceptance for compliance. This is training the child to people please. This may satisfy the controlling parent. However, this is an incredibly destructive personality trait to have out in the world while attempting to operate independently.

People pleasing is a safety mechanism that doesn't work as an adult. It is a direct result from having to contend with control during adolescence. People attempt to please the one who is in control to avoid punishment. This can make a person a potential target for other people in the world to abuse them. People who people please are afraid of what might happen if they acted powerfully. They were usually shut down by authorities before they could ever exert their power fully. This generates a huge fear around authority and personal responsibility. After all, these individuals have been taught it is safer to disengage from power than to use it to be self-supporting.

Being a good parent means being in command of your family without needing to dictate or control what everybody is doing. A good parent generates the energy for self-organized freedom. A good parent knows everyone is responsible for their choices and contributes to the good of the whole. There is a natural consequence for behaviors that cause the system to fall out of order. Healthy structure is what allows a good person who is parenting to be in command. They have structured boundaries that honors everyone. Healthy boundaries allow each individual to enjoy life while keeping them safe and the family system well-functioning.

Having command means being in control of the system from which the individual functions from and not the individual itself.

13

Healthy Boundaries

In order for a family system to work properly it needs to be governed by healthy boundaries. A boundary is created anytime we permit or deny something. A boundary is like an open or closed command on a computer system. Your life is made up of a series of yes or no responses that are governed by your beliefs and personal choices.

When thinking is consistent, boundaries will be consistent. When emotions are all over the places, the choices made will be all over the place too. Behavior is always affected by a belief. If a person believes their child is trying to insult them by defying them then they will act on that belief in behavior that depicts protection. If a person believes people who are late are trying to take advantage of them then they will act insulted. All beliefs result in certain behaviors. Other people's behaviors are a result of what the other person is feeling. Behavior is only a feedback about how a person is responding. People may respond to other people's boundaries as if there is something wrong with them. However, setting a boundary is how one protects oneself. People have to set boundaries or else they allow everyone else make their own decisions.

Having good boundaries comes from knowing what to say yes or no to. A person who doesn't understand their boundaries will be inconsistent with what they say yes and no to. Boundaries are like invisible lines of the self. They protect certain parts of you. Kids are always trying to push boundaries to see who you are, not to make your life difficult. They don't know who they are without the definition of you. An unhealthy family will have inconsistent boundaries with everything. The father may sleep with the daughter. The mother may be in love with another man but still stays with the father. The siblings may be more like enemies than they are comrades growing up independently. People who have poor boundary structures have lives that are going every which way but the direction they really wish to be going. This function is marked by the degree of unhealthy boundaries.

When you set healthy boundaries it takes you to where you want to be going. Healthy boundaries means saying no to unhealthy people and yes to things that are functioning. Parents who don't have very good boundaries can easily lose their temper. People pleasers are more prone to explode. Anytime a person suppresses true feelings the truth builds. The feelings need to come out. This is when people emotionally explode. Anger is a way of projecting, onto another person, what really angers us about ourselves. Unmanaged anger is the number one reason for abuse. Anytime a person displaces anger onto another they need to ask themselves how they are really angry at themselves.

Parents who are in their power feel no need to yell, scream or fight with anybody. They stand congruent in their energy physically, mentally and emotionally. The congruency conveys something of power when they are communicating. This congruency puts a parent in better command because they are consistent in how they are communicating and what they are conveying. Like any leader, a parent must earn the respect of who they are responsible. They do this by commanding the family energy in kind yet firm way.

Parents separate from their power when there are unhealed emotions and abuse. All the unhealed emotional wounds people seem to be suffering creates a demand in our society for healing. Things like emotional chaos, financial problems and relationship difficulties all have the potential to diminish power. Separation from personal power can lead to a series of consequences such as loss of health, poverty and codependence. Healing the relationship you have with your power is essential if you wish to be a solid, loving and effective parent. There are many different support groups to help you rediscover your own happiness.

Parents are leaders to their family. When parents don't lead there will be no structure. A good leader sets boundaries that serve to protect others. What children really wants are good parents to lead them. A good leader brings out the best in others which is the skill required in the seventh stage of parenting. If you are the type of parent who has no structure then this will be very difficult for your children. At some point your children will be formed and you have to let them go, even if they were abused. You have to let them go knowing you did the best you could.

It is never too late to implement this vision you have for your family. No matter how dysfunctional your family may have become, there is always the chance of healing when you do the right thing. Every day you are free to choose what you are creating. Many people spend more time plotting their business goals than they do raising their family. Contemplate what your overall vision is for your family. If you start plotting your vision early then you are most likely to succeed later on. A leader knows he or she can't make anyone do anything they don't want to do. Instead of using manipulation, they use inspiration. When you inspire your family to be their best this is what makes you a good parent. Whether or not they choose to act is up to them.

The mental and emotional health of the individual determines how well they set boundaries so they can flourish in all aspects of life.

14

Unexpected Journeys

Often time's life takes people on a different course then they ever expected. As you have become a parent you may have had to set aside some of your own dreams and ambitions. These freedoms all come back as your child gets a little older if you have put in the time when they are younger.

You don't have a second chance to raise your kids. Nor do you get to go back and live out other missed opportunities. Finding a balance in what you pursue is important. There is always more than enough time for everything when you allow yourself to flow with life. Trust your intuition. The sum of your accomplishments is made up of all the little chunks of time you have set aside for yourself.

Many people look back over their lives and see the mistakes of they have made that have led them to experiences that were not what they wanted. We only have one chance to raise a child and if we do it right we can save our children a lifetime of destruction. However, the soul process of raising a child as a parent is not the only place of influence. We have a society of other kids that they are exposed to. We have other parents who are either doing their jobs or doing our jobs a disservice by neglecting their responsibilities. We have a culture of free will that isn't really respecting authority. We have propaganda waging war politically. There are many things in our 21st-century society that affect our parenting. When we become aware of these factors we can be more educated to do something.

The best way to live life is to always act with the intention of love. When you act with love in your heart you can't go wrong. Follow what your heart tells you to do. If you can't hear your heart, clear out the old pain so you can hear what your heart has to say to you. A person who can't hear their heart is separated from their feelings. Your heart will always lead you the right way. Other people may throw you off course by acting in unloving ways. But when you act with love you come from your greatest power.

When you raise your kids, raise them with love. Love is *always* understanding. Love is always patient. Love always sets boundaries. Love is fun. Love honors everyone. Love knows that everyone is important.

Each member within the family is a key player for success and deserves love equally. Each member should be valued and respected and contribute what they can equally. Any sibling gifts should be balanced and distributed equally, no matter what has been happening. Contributions for any efforts should be clear spoken as to avoid sibling rivalry and any other conflicts.

Each person should have the right to set their own boundaries. Boundaries create freedom and self-respect. Boundaries come from keeping the five freedoms mentioned earlier. To learn more about these freedoms you can read material by David Viscott.

Some children contribute more to the family than other siblings do and yet they receive less recognition in the form of compensation than others do. A parent may pay for one child's education and not the others. These imbalances lead to sibling rivalry and deeper conflicts. It is important for a parent to diminish sibling conflicts by treating each one fairly no matter what.

Not all family members will be treated the same but a fair and just family gives equal opportunity. They do not single out certain family members because of their personality. Parents are human and make mistakes. If a parent more easily identifies with the personality of another child and favors them, this parent is out of balance. Certain members, depending on how large your family is, might receive special privileges that can affect the way other members view this person. These imbalances are sometimes necessary. A child with special needs may need to receive extra attention. However, it may lead to unnecessary resentment if not handled appropriately.

When the psychological pain of life becomes debilitating it is an indicator is it time to clear an old way of thinking.

15

Raising a Child in Abusive Conditions

Raising a child in an abusive household creates a lot of emotional patterns to contend with. A child can instinctively sense whether or not the mother's emotions are welcoming. A mother may reject her child in order to protect herself from painful emotions. A mother with such low self-esteem or trauma will not know how to connect. As a result she will distance herself emotionally. There is abuse in almost every part of the world and yet on some level the abuse always begins at home.

Familial abuse can start to happen at any stage and at any age. Abuse can begin with a mother or father who has the best intentions for their children. We operate from mental programs that are running our lives and some people think it is okay to abuse others to get what they want even though it is not. Parents require healing stages after certain experiences but it is challenging to get the down time because parenting never stops.

A mother can at any time choose to stop her patterns of abusing herself and others by owning her own feelings and finding the right support. This can be an arduous job because it takes a lot of strength to admit and take ownership of personal feelings. The natural tendency is to blame others. Some people are the worst to have to deal with. They can be child abusers, financially vindictive or even rapists. While it is true, other people can make other's lives miserable, it is ultimately up to you personally to find your own inner power to overcome them.

No matter how challenging a situation is, there is always a way. That old saying, "where there is a will there is a way" is true. If you find you are caught in circumstances of any type of mistreatment you must forge ahead and build enough inner power to transcend the conflicts.

The biggest challenge people face with raising kids is how these little people that we love bring up all of their own unresolved feelings. Any deficiency in the form of money, love, emotional deficiency will influence our capacity to give our kids what they need. If we have any stored feelings that we haven't faced it will create emotional responses that affect them in very specific ways.

Some families are dealt a terrible hand of fate. From the very beginning children brought into these types of struggles have a nearly impossible time adjusting to society and living in a successful way. The objective is to be able to raise healthy, happy, well-adjusted individuals who can maintain a fulfilling life for themselves once they leave home. This requires many lessons, experiences and the ability to learn as you go.

Parents have to educate themselves to keep the family healthy. Parents fall short if they are not working each stage mindfully. You only have one chance to raise your child. You don't get a second chance. When you do it right from the very beginning you give your child an opportunity for success. However, there are many factors that play into your child's overall success. You can be the best parent and if you don't have a community that supports you, a family that nurtures you and a spouse that loves you, there will be extra challenges to overcome no matter how great a parent you are.

When people are in abusive situations they can emotionally check out from parenting just to cope. The most challenging thing you can ever do is remain emotionally present to the people you love. If you are in an abusive situation you will naturally begin to check out of life. The longer the stress is endured the more it changes who you are. You check out emotionally from problems in your life. These problems prevent intimacy. You may not have a problem with your child specifically but have a difficult time connecting due to other emotional distractions. Maybe you don't have enough money. Maybe you have plenty of money but don't have loving support from your family. Maybe you love your husband, have plenty of money but have unhealed issues from your own upbringing. The scenarios are endless but chronic stress can prevents intimacy.

If you are in an abusive relationship and it's affecting your kids, you have to find your power to get out. Child protective services and various governmental organizations are not usually the ideal supports that come in and actually protect a child. The political red tape has procedures that may or may not prove to actually protect individual rights of safety. Abusers are very good at hiding. It's up to you to save yourself and take the necessary actions that you can take to make your life and your child's life the best.

If you find yourself in an abusive situation you need to find ways to help yourself. Find the right people who can help you resolve the real conflict. You are your own best advocate. Stay strong and find the right support you can trust so you can get out. Sometimes this means completely clearing out everyone from your life in order to do that.

There are many people who've overcome abuse and so can you if you find yourself in a situation where someone is abusing you. Abusive conditions are collective. Everyone involved becomes a part of them. Even good people support abusers by not saying anything. People who don't take action are actually allowing someone to abuse somebody. A parent who watches another parent abuse their child is passively abusing a child when they do nothing.

People have to be proactive in combating what is happening in today's society. People are becoming more abusive and more controlling and getting away with it because no one's doing anything. Take action and find your power

Dysfunction has to work itself out in a natural way. The dysfunction has to dispel itself until the real self is relieved. We cannot force a system to function differently by applying abuse or manipulating. That is how that system got out of place to begin with initially. What dysfunction needs is for each individual to recognize how they have been operating and seek the help through healthy reinforcement they need so they can operate in a way that is fully functioning.

Emotional release work allows the limbic system to release the feelings that have been blocked. There are a variety of different therapeutic schools of thought. Each one can be effective if they reach the feeling that is causing the mental, emotional or physical problem.

16

Silent Power

When you were raised you had specific needs that were either met or went unmet. A good feeling about your childhood indicates your needs were met. A bad feeling about your childhood indicates your needs were not met. These unmet needs can begin to come up when your child reaches the same age or stage you were when your deficiencies occurred. You can look back over your life and see the same difficult stages in your child's upbringing and know those time periods were probably directly related to your own difficult time periods. The energetic transference of feelings are passed on through our emotional responses. Whatever we suppress our children take on. A parent and child are one and the same. They are always different but always connected. Both parent and child come from a symbiotic union of one from the very beginning. The process of separating occurs throughout each stage of developing.

Abuse is the number one reason for hardships surrounding parenting. Abuse exists at every level of our existence. The basic definition is a lack of respect for anything that is living. Without a developed sense of mindfulness we can unknowingly inflict abuse all of the time. Living abuse free means being around people who have a high regard for life.

Anyone who violates the rights of another is stealing away part of the other person's life. Narcissism and entitlement are huge issues. If you find your children operating like this, then you as a parent need to rein them in. The amount of parents allowing their children overtake others is becoming an epidemic. They don't want to reprimand their child because they think it is abusive. There are fine lines to consider when debating abuse and yet abuse is considered to be anything that diminishes one's quality of life.

Setting boundaries and teaching respect enhances the quality of life. It is just a matter of what you use as a tool to enforce it. If you are using humiliation and shame, this is maybe not as effective as another methods.

A person can be abusive to themselves and as a result it lowers the quality of life, especially for them. Some people would rather abuse themselves than another person because they have been so abused they over empathize with others. They have no sense of self to guard with necessary defenses. If your partner is good to you but abuses themselves through addiction, poverty or negative self-talk, it still lowers the quality of life.

As you met with your partner you most likely formed a union. In abusive relationships there is no real union. The connection is built on power and control. These behaviors are like emotional games people play to manipulate in an attempt to get their needs met. Just like a child's behavior always makes sense, so does an adult's behavior in their relationships. An adult who abuses is no different than a child that abuses. Both are attempting to get their needs met through intimidation and power. Abusive behavior is as if to say, "give me what I need or I will hurt you." Weak people abuse other people. They may be physically strong or financially powerful but inside they are weak.

The biggest challenges in people's lives that influences a person's parenting is being involved with other people who are unloving. There are many people who are inconsiderate of others. They place their inconsiderate behavior onto others making the other person have to bear the emotional weight the other person can't handle. Issues like abuse, abandonment, and chronic lies all impact life in a negative way. Some parents abuse the other parent by withholding from them financially. They have more than enough money to pay for the support of their kids but they choose to not pay it so that it affects the other parent adversely. This is absolute abuse. Parents who do such atrocities should be arrested. And yet they're not. The government allows deadbeat parents. Currently there is just as much dysfunction in the legal system as there is in some families. Any dysfunction at all will influence parenting adversely. The courts can be just as abusive as a terrible spouse. The best thing to do to combat any difficulty parenting is to avoid people who are unhealthy. Avoid liars, cheaters, and jealous people who may try to tear you down as a parent. Do what you can to empower yourself and avoid people who are irrational and narcissistic.

You most likely have a very specific way that you would like to parent. If this approach is healthy and balanced there will still be people who don't like it. People are controlling by nature. People who are in fear control any time they can. There are many people who get triggered emotionally when someone is affecting their parenting. With all the different ways people choose to parent it is almost unrealistic to expect conflicts not to happen.

People who impose their abuse will be most difficult in eliminating. It takes a skilled person who knows how to overcome controlling personalities. Difficulties parenting arise from controlling personalities. If people were more loving they wouldn't even have to contend with half the problems they deal with in society, but they're not. People in general are fear based thinkers who are either greedy or trying to survive. The best thing you can do as a parent is learn how to stay out of the emotional conflict by being in your silent power.

Your silent power comes from knowing who you are without having to say a word. Your silent power comes from observing who people are without feeling the needing to change them. Silent power is knowing when to walk away from an argument or a fight knowing that it will do no good and yet still standing up for yourself by holding your inner positioning. When you are in your power as a parent you are raising your family with love. It doesn't matter who tries to take this away from you, you are going to still do your job. You can face any challenge in life when you have your silent power. You carry this power within you anytime you are silent and communicate more from the place within. You know you are in your power when your boundaries are clear.

People who are asleep are in denial of what is happening. It is through the inability to be honest that hardship enters.

17

Controlling Relationships

There are two types of control. There is passive control which comes in the form of people pleasing and avoiding conflict. This type of control is an attempt to use control to manage control. This occurs when someone control who they are in order to comply to the demands of an overt controller. An overt controller uses direct force to overpower. Overt control can appear as verbal insults, physical punishments or financial withholdings.

Whatever your emotional union is with your significant other affects what you bring to your child. Say you don't have a relationship and you are a single parent. This absence of a relationship affects a child just as much but in less obvious ways. An absence of a parent can lead to feelings of abandonment and emptiness. When you form a happy union you can more easily bring love, affection and attention to your child. This is what everyone is usually trying to do; have the most harmonious relationship they can have. This doesn't occur until you have a healthy relationship with yourself.

If you form a union with someone who does not love you or is mean and abusive, they'll be more difficult to deal with later on as they have gotten used to controlling you. If you suffer from an abusive relationship it can also be more painful to give the tender love to your children. Some people notice they end up confusing the love they need with what they give to their kids or they close off to them. Many people also confuse controlling behavior as power but it is not. Control stifles people. Too much control can cause the family to eventually disintegrate and go their separate ways. Control prevents a soul from creatively experiencing life.

Many siblings when they were younger endured emotional violations that they were not old enough to articulate. These violations create emotional atmosphere towards the other simply as an adult. It takes a lot of healing to link these experiences up with the core self. When the will of a person is violated emotional destruction occurs. The will is connected to freedom of choice to choose and use power the way one wants to. Any violation will stunt a person's emotional growth. A violation causes a person to use their will to protect themselves where they shouldn't have to. It is so important for you as the adult of your kids to make sure they are not violations going on from you or anyone.

You become a controlling parent when you reject or deny your child for what they are feeling. Parents who withhold inheritance or monetary rewards from a child they don't like is manipulating with control. Playing material favorites does deep psychological damage that perpetuates itself. It creates emotional states and financial conditions of imbalance that undermine one's efforts. Yes, every situation is different, yet each child should be treated with monetary equality, because not doing so means the last message that child receives from the parent is one of unworthiness and inadequacy.

Parents can use any medium to be controlling. Physical abuse is exerting physical power to exert control. A parent who emotionally withholds uses emotional rejection to control. A parent who uses money to get what they want uses objects and material withholding to feel powerful over another individual. All are unhealthy attempts to manage their own emotions that they cannot seem to feel. If you can identify with this behavior, it is best to get in touch with what you really feel. When you connect to your own feelings and learn how to meet your own needs through personal power instead of control you will find every relationship in your life working more. You have an actual potential to have your needs met when you let go of any need to control.

No one likes control because it limits the way a person can function. When someone assumes control over you it is because they want to limit you in some way so they can benefit by your altered function. Control is a natural, human tendency. The need to control diminishes as people awaken to their inner power through self awareness rather than controlling things externally.

Control comes from an external source trying to shape you. To give way to control allows something external to define you. The biggest challenge in overcoming control is finding the power from within to be the real you.

Family Dynamics

As a devoted parent it is easy to forget your own dreams. When you lose yourself, you lose your *sense* of self. When you are no longer connected to who you are you are no longer operating fully within the family team. Maybe you are taking on more than your fair share of duties. Maybe you feel unloved and unrecognized for all you do. A family is a team effort which requires a good leader. As the parent, you are the leader. You have to teach self-discipline. You have to stay connected to the truth of what is happening. If you see a misalignment you have to correct it. Every child will come out of a family with some type of emotional issue. It is up to you to minimize it by addressing it before they leave home. Accomplish that, and you'll be ahead of the game.

No matter how loving a person you are, there are always other factors that influence abuse. A large amount of our survival depends upon how we can interact with our environment. We need people to survive. We need love, affection, praise and acceptance. We need to feel we belong to the group. A mother's emotions will give emotional clues as to how her child must become in order to survive his or her environment. A mother may modify her feelings and emotions in order to survive her own environment but a child always the truth of a mother's emotions, even if she hides them. The two are very connected, because the mother is always the primary source of the child's survival.

When the mother does not feel loved, embraced or praised for all she is doing she will eventually develop emotional responses of retreat. When a mother emotionally retreats, her family can start to develop dysfunctional aspects. This affects everybody. The woman should be honored always. We don't always see this in today's society.

There is very little worldly reward for being a good mother. In fact, many people praise outward forms of professional success more than the quiet success that lends itself to life. There is a lot of effort that goes into raising well-adjusted and intelligent kids that go out in society and contribute their good. This lack of recognition is leading to the decline in those who take pride in the role that generates happiness in people's lives.

A mother who is not appreciated will eventually grow resentful and if there is no one around to praise her or give her love. She can take these painful feelings out on the very people she perceives as taking from her; her children. This is how mothers abuse their children. They don't feel loved. They have not dealt with their own emotional problems.

Give love to the woman and everyone flourishes. Make sure the mother has all of her needs met in the family will be a success.

19

Unloving Relationships

If you as a parent are emotionally, financially or attacked by anyone within your sphere of influence, whether it be your mate, ex, family member, or someone in society, it is the child who suffers. A child will be impacted by everything that goes on in the family, especially through observing people he or she loves going through a traumatic experience.

When a family goes through hardship, it affects everyone. The emotionality that develops will be reflected in in the development of emotional problems. A person who develops a strong need to overpower and control everything usually has an upbringing that left them feeling powerless at someone else's mercy. Or, maybe they bonded with their father who was that type of personality and as a result they took on the abusers' characteristics as a means of survival.

A child who endured financial hardship may develop a strong need to amass huge amounts of money. A child who was emotionally abandoned may feel a strong need to nurture everybody. Whatever the case may be, everything that goes on within a family affects the child's emotionality. The relationship that impacts a child the most is the relationship between the couple leading the family.

If you are in an abusive relationship it will impact your ability to parent. When a person is being abused they are in survival. Escaping an abusive situation is nothing more than freeing yourself from the emotional patterns caused by limiting beliefs.

When we are asleep emotionally we close down. We blame others for our own unhappiness because we are not in our power.

Abusive relationships have a way of closing down our power which makes us ineffective parents after a while. You have more influence when you are connected to your power. When disconnected from your power people don't believe you or hear what you have to say. In order to be fully connected to your power you have to be able to back the energy up. When your head, heart and words are congruent, your actions line up.

When people tolerate abuse it is because their true self-worth is incongruent with their inner thoughts of what they are worth. They might believe they are not good enough. They might think if they stay things will eventually get better. Or, they might think their love has enough power to change someone. All of these beliefs are traps that keep people stuck in abusive conditions.

The loss of love generates its own visceral response. Places inside of a person die from abuse because they emotionally disconnect from them. They attempt to look for the bridge that will lead them to the next moment and allow them to arrive safely at what they think they are looking for. What people don't realize is remaining connected to our true feelings is the only thing that gets us to where we want to go.

Abuse of any kind causes people to become emotionally delusional which separates them from actual reality. People who abuse others because of their emotional tendencies are no better than the people who caused the deficiency. When people validate other people's losses without abusing another person for their deficiencies, what people experience is a healing.

Blended families add an additional challenge to harmony because both are usually suffering from their losses silently and incongruently. The emotional nature of two different systems of dysfunction can exacerbate problems. Family losses can cause upheaval in everyone. A family that isn't allowed to feel can't deal. The model for a functional family is one that permits each individual the right to feel as they really do. The leaders in the family have the emotional intelligence to teach the younger ones how to release their feelings in constructive ways. Suppression causes destruction. Creativity releases emotion. A healthy family knows this.

How you emotionally hold yourself in any relationship will give an impression as to how people can treat you. The dynamics you have to contend with are the ones you are not necessarily adept at averting. People who start to blame do so because they can't see their own positioning. Blaming can also be an attempt to set a boundary in hopes someone will hear what they are doing but it is usually an ineffective attempt that changes nothing.

Abusive conditions can be difficult to escape. It takes more power to muster the capacity to leave than to suffer the abuse. When all of our life force is being used to manage someone else, we become ineffective at creating the life we want. Abusive relational dynamics lead people down a path of misery until one finally awakens enough to see how they have been giving their power away for a meager exchange of so called love.

A person becomes free from abuse when they have nothing left to lose anymore. The abuse has eroded away the self enough to where only raw power takes hold. The real self wants nothing to do with the suppression anymore.

Family dynamics of abuse are endless. Some people can do the cruelest things in attempt to relieve the pain stuck inside of them. Statistics show 98% of the time abuse begins with a man. This may be due to the natural tendency for men not to know what to do with their emotions.

A woman is mostly wired to nurture. A man is mostly wired to protect. If he perceives a woman as a threat he can easily attack her unless he becomes more emotionally developed. These levels of emotional intelligence are what affect relational dynamics. Women who abuse are emotionally unintelligent. They are precisely what impact your child's development. No matter how emotionally evolved you are there will always be difficulties to contend with.

Getting out of an abusive relationship requires a power that is at least 2-3 times stronger than the force that is controlling you. This power to pull you out comes from your own volition and the proper support that is equipped to deal with the contending psychological condition.

Abusers are always weak in some area. When you can inform yourself about your abuser you become stronger than them. This means you need the right support to assist you as you get out and a plan of action that allows you to rebuild fast. Most people don't escape because of the amount of energy it takes to break free is enormous. People who escape the binds of abuse find their freedom within and never look back. They find they have more resources because they have their energy back.

An abuser brainwashes their victim into believing they will never make it without them. The abuser never wants the victim to leave. They enjoy the power they get from essentially emotionally owning another person. It isn't easy to break free of the cyclical dynamics that are preventing you from having your freedom.

Finding your power comes from observing your behavior that has formed out of adaptation to the abuser and then breaking those patterns. This can feel strange. You might be taking all the right actions but pretending to respond in your old ways. You are on your way to freedom but you won't be out even once you are out.

Once you think you are free is when the real problems can occur. The abuser does not like it once their victim has left them and they have no one to syphon power from. They no longer turn on the charm. What they do now will be determined by their coping skills and their subset of psychological problems. Freedom comes from doing the work at hand and expecting problems long after the escape has occurred. A skilled professional can help you devise an escape plan. Doing it alone isn't always safe because some abusers have real problems.

There are always opposing forces. A bully uses force to dominate rather than command his or her own energy. They have no inner perspective on life so they fear everything. Whatever they are trying to dominate and overthrow is actually what they fear. Empowerment is the only quality that overthrows control. Control equals helplessness, powerlessness and opposition.

Freedom comes with independence and absence of obligation except to serve the true self which is always some form of love and truth. The opposite of freedom is communism, suppression, subordination, lower rank, feeling less important or inferior.

While escaping any abusive situation, stay focused on the freedom you are about to give your true self by leaving. Once you are out be mindful of who you might commit to and be extra mindful of who you involve yourself with. Create an out for yourself in every involvement. A healthy person won't mind if you need to clarify a plan because they are not secretly planning for entrapment. A controlling person won't like it. They have a special plan for how they want to use you to benefit themselves. If you have an out then they might even be uninterested because where does that leave them? They will feel unsafe with a plan that doesn't ensure they have a victim.

Emotions serve to protect you. Trust your gut intuition. If something doesn't feel good about a situation, always trust it. Your sixth sense is there to preserve your life and offer you your soul's wisdom. Follow it implicitly. It usually only comes in once but will sit there until you hear it. There will always be a risk involved in standing up for what is right but if you don't stand up, the force just gets stronger. People make the mistake of thinking if they please the abuser that he, or in some cases *she*, will let them go. This isn't so. Every time an abuser supersedes the power over another they gain control. People who are in control don't like to let go very easily. They need someone to abuse so they can maintain a particular feeling. They will feel so out of control inside that if they can control you. They don't have to feel how weak they are if they can hold power over you. You take that feeling away and you are going to have every wound they are suppressing pointed right at you.

When you are with an abuser you must question who you are becoming and where your power is going. You only get one life. You have to question if this is really how you want to be living? When you are removing yourself from a destructive situation you must find your power.

Victims cope by abdicating their power. This might seem like a counterintuitive approach to someone who is healthy but to someone who has fallen victim to someone else's abuse this is survival. A perpetrator selects targets based on who is not in their power. Parents who do not empower their kids are setting them up to be abused. A parent who teaches their child how to stand up for themselves against the force of overpowering is giving their child skills for his or her own ultimate happiness.

A community is only as healthy as the people living within that community. To raise healthy children you have to have a healthy family where everyone is free to get what they need.

20

Core Needs

Everybody has a baseline for core needs. When you can acknowledge your true needs then you become resourceful at meeting your child's needs in ways that are healthy. When people can't establish an understanding for what they need they began to act out in behavioral ways that are destructive. It is helpful knowing what these core needs are. One can say people need love but what does love really mean?

Kids form unhealthy habits in order to escape uncomfortable feelings. Addictions with kids form from the lack of love. When there is no love a child feels empty. Whatever their reaching for is an attempt to fill up the emptiness. The only way to solve any problem is through love. What is love though? Love to everybody is different at times. Sometimes love comes in the form of physical affection. Other times love comes in the form of education. Identifying what your child needs in the form of love comes from understanding what they are not getting. If you were to define what your child is not emotionally receiving but needs what would that be? One might even question if they are being a good parent.

As your children get older you will want to ensure they have the capacity to set boundaries with anyone they come into contact with. This will endure their self-preservation. Boundaries are created by the capacity for a person to say yes or no to what they choose. If a person doesn't have their freedom to choose then they don't have the power to make a yes or no decision. The power to choose yes or no is like a rudder to your life; they govern your direction. When you make the choices that feel right from within you usually get closer to where you want to be.

After you and your children understand how boundaries are set then you will want to reinforce them with personal empowerment. A boundary with no power backing is weak. The boundary will do nothing. You want to raise your kids to be strong and to be able to reinforce their choices. Be mindful of how you violate them in their own choices. You as a parents are the key person in their life. How they interact with you will influence how they interact with life. If you honor their boundaries and allow them to assert their authority then they will develop this power to use out in society.

After they have their boundaries in tact you they will need to know how to meet there own needs. There are two different ways of expressing needs. A surface need is something that covers up a deeper unmet need such as I want more money. The desire for more money may come from the inability to express oneself creatively. Giving more money does not necessarily make someone happy. The need for a child to be left alone is not necessarily a need but could be a cover up to something else.

Always identify the two sets of needs in anything they are requesting; the surface need and the deeper need. If you're not sure what your child needs, look at what they are expressing and if you are still not sure, ask them what they feel they need emotionally. Then use your intuitive skills as a parent to navigate this situation accordingly.

Here are some core examples of what everyone needs: Everyone needs to feel liked and approved of. When a person feels rejected they don't feel respected. Not everyone is going to like everyone. It is unrealistic to expect everyone to get along in this world. People need to have their certain groups set up where they can relate and interact the way they want. People who feel rejected don't feel respected and this creates a problem. People need to feel respected. Respect comes from feeling included, wanted and accepted.

The second set of needs come from needing to feel effectual. There is a need for a sense that whatever is sought after in heart and mind can be attained. If a child cannot complete something to satisfaction they won't get the sense of satisfaction that makes them feel effectual.

Children want to see results from their efforts. Children also want to feel needed, wanted and appreciated. This gives them self-esteem. All kids naturally want to contribute to the family, but not in families where parents are controlling. They will need to participate in contributing t the good of the whole to meet certain emotional needs. The more you celebrate what family means the more you will find your kids contributing to the good of the whole naturally.

Your child also has a need for clarity. They want to know who is in control, who is in command and they want to know what will be happening next. If they don't get the sense of connection it might be hard for them to regulate their activities. They also want to feel in command and control of their own lives. If you as a parent over controls your child they are not going to get the need for effectualness met.

A child will feel more effectual when they feel heard. They are always communicating to you what is happening even if they are not saying it directly with their words. Their behavior is their language. If they have an attitude they are usually trying to protective by being defensive. If they think everything is "uncool" it is usually because they are trying to create their own persona. If they are deeply depressed it is because some extreme needs have not been met. When they are happy it is because they have their needs met; they have parents who love and support them, minimal conflict, friends they can related with and a life that feels good to them.

Each child's capacity for communicating is different. Not all kids feel like communicating excessively but they do want to communicate. When you take the time to hear them they feel heard. This meets an important need. It also leads to another need of them feeling attached. All kids need to feel connected to something. When you take the time to hear them they bond. This bond helps open you up for better rapport for parenting.

A child has a strong need to feel loved, admired and cherished. When you take the time to treasure who your child really is and what they represent it makes them so happy. Take the time in a relaxed way to indulge in their uniqueness. Be sincere and open. When you can bring out the best in your child it's because your authentic. You're appreciating who they are and they feel admired for it. This meets a huge need that everybody has but when you do it to your child they will fill relaxed, successful and become prosperous because you support them. When they go to direct their energy they know it's valuable because it's already been shown to them. Kids don't know these feelings unless there given to them. You give your kids tremendous value when you admire them.

Kids have a need for cleanliness, beautiful places, may even want to travel and see the world so they feel connected to something greater. Not all families have the capacity to do this but they can always keep a clean home so their child feels good about where they are. Kids like the feeling of cleanliness, organization and being responsible for basic duties that contribute to this type of thing.

Kids have a strong need for physical affection. A child needs to be touched in the appropriate way 12 to 15 times a day for healthy brain development. Many kids don't get the tactile sensation in the form of appropriate physical affection they need.

They may cause them to develop relational fears and social awkwardness in relating. Touch helps develop the nervous system and soothes people emotionally. Good touch helps people feel secure and safe. It reassures someone that they are cared for by setting them at ease. Appropriate times for affection are important as kids get older. They don't want hugs and kisses in front of their friends.

Kids have the need to feel strong and victorious. On some level they want to creatively perform and bring their inner selves out. The more you prepare them for potential ways people express jealousy the can master the own self-expression. Parents that continuously critique their children are usually insecure themselves. If you critique or make fun of your child they will shut down. Allow your children's verbal and physical expressions to be noticed. Cheer them on and become their best advocates for success.

No matter how much money you have you can meet most emotional core needs with your own relational interactions. Do things that feel good to you. Be around people who make you feel happy. The healthier you are the healthier your children can be. What you're doing when you parent like this is giving your children the opportunity to live the life they want to be living. Meet as many basic needs at home. Do it in a way where they feel emotionally secure and as they develop they will become powerfully secure in themselves. Your role as they become grow older will then be to watch them flourish.

Parenting is a skill that requires so much strength and love that when you master it you feel transformed. You as a parent have a core need to see your children do well and to know you have done a good job. If you miss out on that opportunity then you don't get to realize how effectual, powerful, loving and capable you are.

Your good life begins with being a good parent. Parents who do not get the help they need to be the kind of parent they wish they were being can cause them to feel regret for their legacy. You can always take the time to repair what needs to be repaired in order to be the best parent you can be. Treat your kids the way you would want to be treated if you were them. They are your mirrors for how you have parented them. When you give them the love they need, you heal.

Rejecting your kids does nothing positive, for them. Loving them does everything. Be as loving as you can to these precious little people you are raising and watch your life flourish! What you give out, always comes back. The secret to a good life is being an excellent parent.

Your parenting style has to do with your personality style and your own upbringing. You were raised in a particular emotional style. Your family held certain values and attitudes that influenced you. As you parent these same influences come through.

Conclusion

Being a parent is one of the most difficult roles you'll ever participate in. However, it can also be the most rewarding thing you do if you approach it from the perspectives of love and strength, not in hopes of instant gratification but of learning, as a person. Your child is your mirror. They are only reflecting who they have become, as a result of being a part of your life.

You can manage emotional difficulties any time you enter them with emotional intelligence. Your goal in life is to be as balanced and empowered as you can. If you have emotional programs running that give way to behavioral give way to your own behavioral difficulties, then you will have a challenge parenting, but there is always help for these challenges.

Far too many parents try to cover up their deficiencies and try to be perfect. When in actuality parenting is a process. It is natural to make errors. It is actually part of the evolution of growth. If you were perfect from the beginning you would have no room for growth. Being a good parent means learning to change what doesn't work. People are incredibly resilient. At any moment there is an opportunity for healing. The only way to be strong is to accept your weaknesses.

The most challenging thing to do is to remain emotionally present to the people who are around you. Emotional connections can be filled with dysfunction or with a lot of pleasure. How you use your power is entirely your choice. One of the biggest challenges people face with raising kids is the one we face, when these little people that we love bring up our own inner challenges. Any deficiency in the form of money, love, emotional deficiency will influence your capacity to give your child what they need. When you are emotionally empowered you can transcend these difficulties and become resourceful at problem solving.

There will always be problems to contend with. Your happiness comes from making the choice right now in this moment to emotionally connect and be there for your child. Your life has value. As an adult you can validate your own words. You don't need anyone to do this for you. Move forward in the direction of your dreams. Overcome power struggles and exposure to destructive things. Organize your life in a way that is fulfilling. Make choices that give you what you need. When you are happy as a parent you can give your kids more of what they need.

You may even want to be prepared to feel regret, because there are many things you will do, as a parent, that you will wish you hadn't done. When you look back over your life, you will probably wish you had made different choices. You might even realize that you have rationalized pain and perhaps even a damaged self-image. All of this can be healed, if you are open.

Your life is valuable and has tremendous meaning. Honesty is the easiest way to heal anything. It takes a lot of courage to admit your real feelings. Fears under pressure are almost always expressed as anger that has affected the way you have chosen to raise her children. Taking action on your own healing is the best thing you can do for your child right now. Your own healing is going to be a journey that influences them.

It doesn't matter what you are facing; emotional codependency in relationships, control issues, addiction, and or abuse, when your child sees you recover they develop a championing spirit for you. The best thing you can do, for the people who love you, is to realize your dreams.

To be a great parent you are going to have to overcome many of the fears and misunderstandings you have about the relationship you have with yourself and with each one of your children. You will most likely be forced to evaluate your self-defeating behaviors in your life and your relationships so you can be the best parent you can be. You can use this relationship with your child to love them and heal fully. There is something remarkably rewarding when you make it past the finish line and your young adult is flourishing.

Any upsets or disappointments about your child might be valid and yet a lot of the responses are all projections. A person projects their feelings onto another person when they are out of touch with what they are actually feeling. The more you stop projecting any of your feelings onto your child the more fulfilling the connection will be. Learning to take emotional responsibility and give them their individuality will be very empowering, for your child. You might even see your life in all other areas begin to open up and blossom exponentially.

As you and your family take the time to plot your course for a specific legacy, be open to each other and work as a collective team. Life can be an exciting journey. If you can see yourself as a parent without the need to fabricate anything, then you are standing your power. Some families are dealt a terrible hand by fate. They may never have the chance to fully operate. They may even separate and go different ways. Sometimes these things happen. You can always form a new family with friends you have chosen.

Not all families flourish. Some individuals never serve each other. The lessons are learned through conflict and then they separate. Yet even conflicted families have their own beauty. Your family is your legacy. It is the emotional imprint you leave on the world. Do your best to learn all you can to make sure it is a good one.

What makes a really good parent is the willingness to reveal creativity. People choose love when they choose to create. When you allow your child the freedom of their creative expression you allow the innocence from their soul to move forward and create their destiny. The emotional impurities that stay stuck within the self, impact creativity. Creative expression is the best way you can release these emotionally harmful energies. Help your child find healthy outlets for all that they are feeling. Develop an emotionally pure relationship with your child who is developing. Be willing to make life an exciting adventure. You only get to parent them once so put in your best efforts. Be the type of parent you've always wanted to be. Organize your life however you have to in order to get to that place of feeling.

Love is the greatest secret to any family. It is with love people find they can do anything. Parent from love in your heart and let the natural evolution of life take care of everything. Intimacy is what everyone craves but is afraid of entering. The exposure of revealing your true self and the hope that it will be handled with care by the person to whom you reveal it is seen by our psyche as one of the most intense threats. Some people have no fear in revealing who they are and yet the overexposure isn't safe.

The only reason why we close down in our relationships is because we find them emotionally unsafe. When you expose your family secrets and start learning how to feel you become emotionally powerful. Parenting is challenging because you can easily check out but stay in the game. Be there for your kids in as many ways that you can. You can move through any parental challenge because you have a love inside of you that transfers to them. Choose to be the best parent you can be and watch the self-organizing power of this intention create a familial life that is deeply rewarding.

Anything can be used like a drug. Sex, love, food or actual drugs can act like a false stimulation for the type of unmet needs they are suffering from. Find a way to have all emotional needs met and your child won't have to form an addiction to any type of substance. They will simply know how to move through life getting their real needs met.

Question & Answers

My child is already so closed down, emotionally. Where do I start?

Kids that are closed down emotionally need the people around them to notice them. They needed people to respond to their feelings a long time ago and for some reason they didn't get it. This is one of the major reasons why children close off emotionally; they don't feel safe to expose their true feelings.

Children feel happy when they are seen and recognized in a positive way. If something traumatic occurred, and is still being processed, children can become emotionally closed off. The longer their feelings go unrecognized, the more it increases the chances for mood-swings and other mental imbalances, which is often times nothing more than an engrained behavioral response from unmet needs. The imbalances are usually due to the inability to identify personal needs and emotionally self-regulate harmoniously.

Typically, a person who is emotionally closed down needs to be noticed for what their needs are and what they are feeling. The problem is, these unmet needs develop defensive behaviors that are intended to keep people out. People, including children, build these defenses out of necessity to avoid the pain from being excluded emotionally. These emotional barriers are an attempt to distance and self-protect from others intruding.

Recognizing the true feelings of these types of people is difficult because they use mood swings to separate you, from who they really are, and what their real self is feeling. If you—as a parent with a child like this—can look you can observe their actions, you can then begin to surmise what they might be feeling. Based on what they are doing you can begin to understand the unmet needs based on how they are behaving. This is big because it will allow you to love them in a way that serves them.

As you identify their true feelings by following their patterns of behavior, you can then be that mirror that helps reflect back to them what you are seeing. Once you have identified what they might be feeling, you can make a neutral statement about what you are observing. This might sound something like, "I notice you haven't gotten your school work in on time this week. Is there something going on personally?" Linking a non-judgmental observation with a question can help open the doors for communication.

If people don't want to open up it is unrealistic to expect them to do so. Closing off emotionally has to do with feeling unsafe in opening to the person who is trying to connect with them. The best way to build this rapport is through emotional trust that you give them. Remain as consistent as possible with your own emotions. Also, give them the recognition they need to feel truly valued. If they can get emotional relief through your positive recognition, they will be more likely to open up and feel more relaxed emotionally.

True validation helps relieve emotional tension. Closing down emotionally is an unconscious behavioral response that becomes a habit intended to self-protect from being emotionally rejected or denied validation. This is when cycle of negative behavior begins—in an attempt to receive any type of recognition.

Any child with extremely poor behavior is attempting to slough off the pain of invalidation. Behaving poorly is a means for validation that they exist. It is driven by anger for people not noticing them. Acknowledge who they are. Validate their true feelings and recognize them for their genuine efforts. Then you will have a child who will want to start to open up.

A child who is emotionally closed can only open up when given enough positive reinforcement and emotional consistency to make it possible. Parent's need to be aware of their own mood swings because any inconsistencies can cause your child to close down emotionally.

To help your child open up emotionally, give them positive attention that tells them that they exist. They can feel mortified when people notice them in a not-so- positive way. It is easy for a kid to feel humiliated when their parents point out things about them to others. The same thing happens when they are recognized in a positive way. They light up and feel alive. It's because someone sees them inside. Kids don't know they exist unless they are witnessed.

The more you as a parent can be sensitive to your child's personal space, feelings and life the more they will invite you in because they will trust you are safe.

If your child reaches for you and you respond, what you are actually doing is building a bond. If you didn't build a bond with them early on by forming a genuine connection with them, they will most likely be detached emotionally. A bond helps give the child mirroring that they need so they can experience their inner self that is developing. They do not know what they are feeling unless their feelings are acknowledged. A child who does not have their feelings acknowledged grows up in emotional hiding. What this means is they are uncomfortable connecting with people emotionally.

How can I help my child? He's so shy!

Emotional hiding occurs for many reasons. Shyness is a behavior that comes from the feeling that a person would literally die if they were to show the world who they really are. Some children do not feel safe enough to interact with other people socially. For whatever reason they find certain people's energy intimidating. These insecurities can develop after being part of an abusive dynamic and or from seeing what happens to other people when they are emotionally exposed.

Several things can contribute to shyness and it is not always about what the parent is doing wrong. However, children are less likely to reach outside of themselves to get what they need if their basic needs are not being met from their parents. If a child feels they can't ask for what they need from their parents they will feel unsafe asking for any kind of approval from others. This can lead to very big problems such as poverty, under-earning or health issues all related to shyness and insecurities.

A child who feels safe socially and emotionally will have a better chance at getting needs met when they leave home. Children who aren't socially developed enough will feel unsafe out in the world and, perhaps, will never leave home. Parents can help their children to feel socially safe by encouraging safe situations in which they can interact at their own level of comfort. Forcing your child to interact or get involved only exacerbates fear. Being there for your children, no matter what their ages, and allowing them to participate as they choose instills greater confidence.

The thing to remember is ultimately, every child wants to get involved in life because it is fun. When they feel they have a say over their level of involvement they feel more secure. A sense of security leads to an emotional demeanor that will allow them to be more proactive in their involvements. If a child does not feel emotionally secure then they will choose not to engage.

A developing child's needs are very basic. All children, no matter what age, need love. They thrive on interaction with caring people, and most likely want the emotional connection they are separated from. You can help your child be identifying what is troubling to them in their connection with you and begin to work on improving this aspect too. Do your best to make their real self feel safe so it doesn't have to hide.

Besides blowing a fuse or becoming complacent, how do I handle my child coming in after curfew?

When people are disconnected from their feelings they start getting anxious, upset or even volatile. Most likely you are getting worked up because you have a variety of feelings; scared, mad, annoyed, irate, concerned, etc. Knowing what you are feeling can help you act from a place of calm, collected power. This way when they do come in you can say what you need to say to them. You can set a boundary and perhaps even enforce a consequence.

A parent who blows a fuse with anger might be making the situation more about how they feel than what is actually happening within the overall situation. And that might be part of the problem. The real rage might be that you don't feel your words are respected. In which case, when your child comes in after curfew, do some self inquiry and ask yourself how does it make you feel? Knowing how you feel you can automatically put yourself in a place of calm because you are connected to our feelings.

A child coming in late is about you but it should be more about letting them know this is not okay. When you are acting on their best interested rather than your upset emotions, you will be able to hold your ground and be more effective. After you have identified what you are feeling, you can then be more effective in enforcing the right consequence.

Coming home after curfew is a lot like speeding. Almost everybody does it. It's not what you're supposed to do. It doesn't make them a kid bad, but it is not what they should do. You want to teach them to respect other people's boundaries. Address the real issue and then let it go.

Make sure you are not setting limits, just to be controlling. Make the curfew reasonable. Set a consequence in your mind beforehand while you are calm—one that you can enforce if they should break curfew. Some parents may choose to take away certain privileges because their teen values freedom. Make sure what you take away is linked to a natural consequence and not a severe punishment. Only use extreme consequences when they have really crossed the line with something.

Always consider the real problem and address the actual conflict. Navigate this conflict as you would any other relationship, with calm emotion and diplomacy. The more you deal with your children as if they are young adults, the more they will act like young adults. If you revert back to the old behaviors of screaming or yelling or becoming submissive and quiet, they will not respect you. Remain in your power by staying calm. Keep consistency with your consequences. Maybe they are coming in after curfew because have not paid attention to when they got home, anyway.

Some parents find it helpful to look at situations as business deals: You have a rule. They are required to follow it. If they don't follow it, there is a consequence. The consequence has to match the violation. If the consequence exceeds the violation your child will lose respect for you. If the consequence is too weak and does not match the violation, they will also lose respect for what you want them to do. As an adult and parent set boundaries and stick to them. Keep your word. Be consistent. And approach any conflict with the idea in mind that you are there to resolve it, not to create another one.

There are many concerns for a parent when their child doesn't come in on time. With kids who are typically good, a lot of the time they were just having fun and were not ready to come home. However, if they do this often it's because they don't respect you as the parent. By the time your children go out on their own, they have already developed a mental capacity for living their life and making their own choices. At this point, what you are seeing is the way they make choices *against authority*. First, consider how you are an authority figure in their life. Are you overbearing and unrealistic? What is the curfew limit? Who are you setting the curfew for, you or them? Are they of responsible nature or they mature?

The fact is, your children are going to go out, and while living under your roof they are to follow your rules. This is a healthy and normal part of life. If you set rules that are unrealistic, know that your child is going to resist. You may have your rules but how you enforce them is what gives you the power as a strong leader. A very good leader will allow the people they lead their own free will. Your child is ultimately allowed to break the rules. However, a very good leader will always have a natural consequence for one who breaks their rules and as a result the leader holds power without having to violate anyone's free will.

You as a leader have control over how your household functions. Your rules are part of your jurisdiction. You can put in place any rule you wish as long as it doesn't violate someone's five freedoms and you are humane in your consequence. If your rules are clear and they come from a place of integral power, then your children will want to obey your rules because of the benefits they receive from operating the way the leaders have requested. When you give someone else their own power to choose what they will do, you remain in your power and they do to. If you demand this be their code of conduct and use control and manipulation when they come in after curfew, then maybe you need to look at your own control issues.

Being in command of the situation by staying calm gives you power. If your children come in past curfew first asked them what happened. Maybe they have a good reason for coming in late. After you find out the nature of the situation you can enforce the appropriate and consistent consequence. Maybe they will miss out on going out next week. Whatever you do, stay calm and enforce your rules. Stay in your power. Explain to them why it is important to you for them to come home when you say it is time. A child who can follow simple guidelines will ultimately have more success in life.

How do I handle my adult children not speaking?

Children choose to shut down their communication for a variety of reasons. Some children feel that, if they speak up for themselves they will only be met with more defeat. Other children refuse to speak because it's a way for them to gain emotional power and control. This is a control tactic they have usually learned from observation.

Refusing to speak never helps anyone. If someone is refusing to speak it is usually because they're angry. Pushing for them to speak usually only makes it worse. You may question why they are so angry but they still, may not tell you. Fishing around for what they might be angry about can annoy them, but it is also a way of opening up communication if it is done subtly.

People who have a difficult time opening up may voice resentments one is unprepared to hear, once they do open up. Take in what they say but don't take personally. Someone who has been closed off emotionally for quite some time does not have the skills to open right when someone wants them to. They actually have to gear themselves up for a conversation and they aren't always eloquent. If they have been emotionally removed, they can be out of practice in emotionally expressing their real feelings in any given moment. The more you can just listen and try to understand where they are coming from, the easier it will be to decipher the meaning behind their words they are directing at you.

Children learn communication skills from what they've observed in you and the other people around them. To understand why they are doing this, you may want to ask yourself why the people around you might be doing this? If you behave this way you may want to ask yourself why *you* would be refusing to speak? Was their something that just occurred that caused them to retreat? If so, what just happened? Why might they be feeling scared? Try to find out what is happening inside them when they behave like that by asking them questions that will help them pinpoint their feelings, for example, "Do you feel hurt when someone talks to you like that?"

Parents expect their kids to be able to communicate to them at the same skill level they, themselves, communicate. Some children communicate at a higher level than their parents as adults. But when they are young, they need to be taught. The thing to remember is there will always be an age gap. There will always be the parental/child dynamic. Seeing beyond this is very difficult for the mind. Good communication skills helps to close this gap.

Parents think that because their children look like adults they should be able to communicate like them. This isn't always so. Good communication comes from a healthy household that takes the time to share, takes the time to listen and values everyone's input and perceptions. Children that close off and stop communicating usually do so because they don't know how to articulate what they are feeling or because they feel like it is hopeless. Probing for an answer can work if you are mindful of your children's boundaries.

If you have played an unhealthy role in your child's life all you can do is heal yourself and be open and receptive to who they are today. If you played the role of the person who abandoned them, then they need to find their own healing. Find out why they are so angry. If there has been a history of toxic exchange, all you can do to help them heal is provide the truth so they can reconcile their own pains and move into a place of understanding. This can only come from good communicating. There will be no undoing or trying to replay events that have already been acted out. If they have a deep-seated problem they will have to find their own strength to work this out on their own.

The person who has inflicted the wound often times has not evolved enough to mend the wound or, they retrigger the memory of the wound for the other person and are ineffective at resolving the conflict due to the other person's association towards them. This is when outside help can be helpful. Having a mediator that is an advocate for both people is helpful. This is where some counselors fall short though; they don't always have the ability to distance themselves from taking sides. This comes out in their practice.

In order for counseling to be effective, both sides must be heard. This can be difficult for people who haven't known how to effectively separate out their roles as parent and child. Many conflicts with children who are now adults are still wounded as a child but now they have adult power and are not happy with what happened. Tempering this anger can only come from being a parent that listens. Going back and trying to fix things can't happen. If you put in the time to hear your children's point of view, what you get is an excellent mirror of you. Their perceptions hold a piece of truth, even if they do not seem all the way accurate to you.

Good communication comes from taking the time to hear what people and your children and what they have to say to you so it doesn't all come out years later. Remember, your child is your emotional mirror. They are only responding to something you are communicating or have communicated when they close down to you. Knowing how you are being perceived while you are communicating is helpful in actually resolving the real relational issues. This can only be done when you have dealt with your own wounds and have become emotionally neutral.

If your adult child or teen isn't speaking to you just try to understand where they are coming from. Far too many parents try to cover up their deficiencies and try to be perfect. When in actuality parenting is a process. You will make errors in this connection that may sometimes lead to them refusing a connection. Just remain as loving as possible to yourself and to them.

Sometimes periods of emotional separation are needed for growth. Just remain open and receptive by being willing to keep the lines of communication open. If you identify your faults and openly acknowledge them, this can open the doors to better communication.

How do I handle my kids fighting?

Children are naturally learning how to work out conflict all of the time. If they are not given the right social skills, they fight and they do it in a really obnoxious way. When children are not permitted to stand their ground in a disagreement they do not learn how to stand up for themselves later on in life. When your children fight you may want to identify the real conflict there arguing over. If there is sibling rivalry the conflict will be hard to identify. There is usually resentment from one child towards another about the unfairness they feel comes from another parent. The other sibling may be favored more, and gets in trouble less, and these emotions build up causing unidentifiable conflicts.

To help resolve kid's fighting, recognize it as necessary but then teach them how to argue effectively. Teach your kids good communication skills so they will have more ability to articulate their feelings rather than just fight. They have to learn how to effectively stand their ground while learning how to fight fair, which is an entire subject in and of itself.

The thing to remember is conflict is a very natural part of life. Siblings are going to fight. Teach them how to talk out their real feelings by having them state how they feel. If the person they are sharing their feelings with has any emotional intelligence at all, they will know how to respond. You are trying to teach your children how to identify the behavior that contributed to the bad feelings and then suggest the resolution that would relieve the tension. This is usually some type of boundary or clarification.

It's never too late to learn how to communicate. When children have the right skills they can argue intelligently. Disagreements are a natural part of life. When people don't or can't address conflict, their needs remain unmet but suppression occurs in order to cope with the painful feelings. This suppression leads to a lot of passive aggressive behaviors people don't even know they are expressing.

Holding feelings within creates an inner conflict. Many people misuse their negotiating skills and create an even greater conflict. The energy of emotion can then build up in the nervous system. The key to resolving any type of fighting is getting feelings out and having healthy boundaries set. When people no longer feel the need to violate another person's boundaries, suddenly the relationship starts to work and the other person is no longer feeling angry.

Children with all sorts of pent up emotions can have a lot of frustrating emotional challenges. They can't ground their real feelings enough to make what they want happen. This creates more emotional frustration and even health problems because they feel ineffectual to make anything happen. They are not relaxed. As a result, they have frustration.

You as the parent are always the mediator. Pay attention to the boundaries that each child is setting when fighting for within a conflict. Clarify what they are saying by stating the boundary you see them trying to make. Be fair and emotionally detached. You are there to monitor how communication styles are used to resolve the conflict. But, they must be taught! You can't expect kids to know how to do this on their own.

Take a timeout and help each one of them articulate their feelings, unmet needs and help them set boundaries that protect each individual. Allow each child to stand up for him or herself without violating the rights of others. This will take time but in the end it will create a lot more harmony for you and your family.

I thought I was a good parent. Why is my child getting involved with drugs?

When children are involved in drugs it's because they're looking for some alternate escape from their reality. People who involve themselves with substances to get an emotionally altering affect are actually looking for love they can't seem to get. Kids get depressed more often than adults might think. Drugs provide an emotional outlet for their feelings when no one is listening.

A deficiency in any type of love will create a longing. There are a variety of drugs that produce different types of feelings. Each drug simulates a different kind of mental state that stimulates them emotionally. What the drugs do to the overall state of mental function are incredibly destructive. Kids are young and they don't always understand the consequences of what will happen to them.

As a parent, you need to reach your child's mind first, before someone else approaches them. Their mind is a blank canvas unless you teach them. If someone is chronically lonely and left emotionally abandoned and someone comes around and offers a drug that will help them feel better, who wouldn't try it? Some kids don't. Many kids do, especially when they are misguided and completely disconnected from any type of love whatsoever. What they don't realize in their time of despair is the door to destruction they are opening that leads to nowhere.

Emptiness and loneliness are painful. Drugs are an attempt to fill that hole. Give your kids the love they need before they start reaching for substances such as drugs, sex or alcohol. The process of addiction eventually takes over if you don't intervene and get them help.

The problem and challenge with getting help is, the real problem took root, most likely, when they were preverbal. This means at an age when they couldn't communicate whatsoever. Their development level must exceed their current emotional awareness level in order to develop the power to overcome any addictive pattern that has taken hold. Addictions occur because they don't feel whole. Usually what is required to develop this sense of wholeness is a treatment program that simulates the developmental process as an adult.

The best thing you can do for your addicted child is to maintain healthy boundaries and love them until they feel whole and complete as an adult. There is something going on within them that isn't allowing them to feel powerful on their own. They are now linked with something else that gives them the sense of feeling whole. This is very challenging if they are already an adult.

After a certain age, you are done parenting them. If they are 36 and still drinking, you can't get retrain them because they are already past the necessary developmental emotional stages. All you can do really is listen and support them. Implement tough love with them and teach them the healthy correlation between their choices and their consequences without trying to rescue them. And have faith they have a power inside of them that can change their course of action once they choose to do so.

You as the parent have to make sure your role is a healthy one and that you are not enabling their addiction. You alone are not equipped to handle healing an addiction and here is why. The primary reason the addiction developed in the first place was due to past imbalances. If the problem originated within your household because of imbalanced emotional functions, it is not always effective to play the role of a therapist. If you try to play the therapeutic role but you are not healthy and whole, this only perpetuates the addictive cycle.

The family dynamics they are involved in need to facilitate a healthy functioning support system. The best thing to do if you find your child has an addiction is to reach out for support right away and identify the flaws in your family's emotional functioning.

Healing addictions is a very tricky process that requires an inordinate amount of emotional intelligence to overcome. This may come in the form of professional help. It may come through a twelve step program or it may come through the self. However it comes, the faster the solution arrives the better it is for everyone's life.

Addictions lead to massive amounts of destruction. Tackle them before they become a ginormous monster. It can sometimes take awhile to find the support source that is effective. Not all counselors are appropriate for your child. Find one that works. Heal all feelings of blame and resentment. This will only cause you to lose power. Accept this experience as a part of life and do what you can to correct it.

When your child has an addiction, *you* have a problem. Focus on resolving the imbalances within you that created the atmosphere that was imbalanced for them and work on healing until there is resolution and the problem is solved. All problems have solutions. Your child is perfectly capable of having a good life. People are resilient.

I don't trust some of my kid's friends. What is the solution?

Some parents find they don't care for their children's friends. This is not uncommon. By the time your children are is young adults you really cannot pick their friends. Their preferences are already formed. You can influence their choices by the way you assert your opinions, yet ultimately the decision is theirs.

The best thing to do is to ask them what they see in that particular friend that attracts them to that type of friendship. When you can understand what they get then you can understand why they are choosing it. If they are choosing it but not wanting it, there may be some lack of self-confidence in standing up for themselves.

Solutions come from answering questions. The more you ask your children questions about what they see in a particular friend, the better they can begin to think for themselves about why they are involved in that particular relationship.

Evolved children are those who can make educated choices for themselves. The more you ask them questions without insinuating anything negative, the more they can process their own ideas to think for themselves. If you just dictate who they can or can't be with this teaches them nothing.

Your main objective as a parent is to help your kids know how to navigate the circumstances of their lives. As we know, every connection we have influences our life. We know the importance of trustworthy, good friends. If your child gets burned by a particular friend you may have warned them about, don't say "I told you so." Offer them empathy and ask them what they learned about it. If they are picking friends that in your opinion are not right, consider what might be emotionally driving them towards these personality types.

Your children may or may not yet have the wisdom to answer these questions right away but the question itself causes them to think about it. Keep in mind to not go too far with the inquiring. Over questioning may cause them to close off and become unreceptive. Just know your child hears everything you are saying even if they seem to not be listening. Not listening is different than not acknowledging. Just say what you need to say and then watch how they begin to make their choices.

When you have the urge to dictate who they can or can't, see, put yourself in your child's shoes. What if they told you that you couldn't see certain friends that you knew? In fact, many kids don't like their parent's friends. Parent's friends can be incredibly minimizing, critical and sarcastic. Their parents may brush it off as if that is nothing.

Your child's peers and chosen friends are a reflection of what is taking place within them. Give them enough freedom to make their choices to see what they do. The objective is to get them to see on their own what you do. Barging in and making the choice for them loses the affect. Criticizing them directly does nothing to correct the problem either.

All things considered, who your child permits into their life affects you as well. You have every right to make a decision that you do not want a certain person in your home. You can set this boundary without anyone knowing it is because you don't' trust a certain person. Or, you can come right out and say your true feelings but in a way that honors everyone. For example: "The last four times they were over, something got broken. You guys need to find someplace else to hang out." There is no judgment or blame in that statement, just a simple truth of observation. This is communication for emotional intelligence.

The bottom line is kids have sense of who they do and don't want to be around. They may not know why though. If they are making poor choices it is because they are not seeing the potential problems that come from being affiliated with certain people. The goal is not to instill fear but rather cognitive decision making. Who your child is connected to is going to affect their future. You see it. Now you need them to get it so they can make the best decisions possible. Teenagers should be aware of whom they are choosing to hang around with. If you are dictating who they can and cannot see then maybe they haven't been inspired to make good decisions naturally.

Make seeing the potential problems with certain friends the objective instead of telling them who they can and can't be around. Make sure you are accurate in your assessment before you pre-judge someone. Ask yourself what is the proof in your opinion? Are their solid facts or are you basing your opinion off of assumption? Then ask your child what benefits they get from being around a certain person. Create a clear understanding as to which people you permit into your child's life, and why. When they understand the full picture they are more easily inspired to make decisions that contribute to a good life.

If you would like to explore this concept deeper I would recommend a book I have written about understanding the dynamics of friendships. It is called *The Color of Friendship*. It discusses how each friend has a different color hue. Depending on how the colors mix shapes you. This could be a good book to have your child read to help them understand more how certain friends influence them.

How do I handle my spouse undermining what I'm trying to do with our kids?

It is not uncommon for a single parent to raise children alone today. Parents need to educate themselves and remain connected to their children and other people who support them. Challenges that arise from the lack of love and support cause added pressures to the successful outcome of childrearing.

Parents who are not working well as a team, especially when each uses different methods of childrearing, have added challenges. Continuing changes in family structure are altering the emotional health of both parents and children. This poses an added threat to children who are in the process of coming of age and trying to develop their own security.

Children have many needs that can only be met by each parent individually. If there is anything lacking, it will still affect them no matter how well intended the other parent is. Children need a loving family structure and connections to all aspects of a healthy community. They need to feel safe at home. They need to know they have a family that cares. They need a school that allows for that freedom. They need to feel like a valuable asset to the family. These things come more easily when all both parents and step-parents are involved whole heartedly.

Destructive behaviors such as drugs, addiction, violence and poverty are taking over as wholesome creative exchanges are diminished. The situation with our youth today in some ways constitutes an emergency. Unhealthy parents are raising kids that are even unhealthier. Many children are entering adulthood confused and unable to thrive, because they lack adequate love and support in their lives. The fact is, they were not given the appropriate skills to thrive. This ushers gives government an excuse to come in and control people, when what we really need is a solid family structure.

Some kids have everything handed to them and have no idea about real life or how to survive. Then there are kids who are neglected—just left alone to figure out life. Both sides are imbalanced. Everyone needs to know how to work for a living. Everyone needs to know how to be good to others. Everyone needs to follow their passions and at least attempt their dreams. If a person strikes it rich or gets lucky, he or she will at least know how to survive.

In today's culture of success and material pursuits many parents feel a sense that something is missing. The piece that is often missing is the reassurance that their child is going to grow up and thrive. There are so many challenges in the 21st century that threaten wellbeing. One very significant one is the loss of the traditional family unit. All parents want to know their children will grow up and be able to handle life. On an intuitive level, some people can sense family and community slipping away, and understand the significance of this vast societal change. As the use of technology increases the importance of real human interaction seems to be waning. If the family concept continues to lose its grip, the loss will only ensure that more hardship than happiness comes to define the human experience.

Genuine happiness comes from a solid self-concept. This means knowing who you are and who you are not. A family gives children the concept of who they are. When children are depressed it is because they don't like who they are. The perception they are getting back is formed by the societal responses. The feedback from the world around them influences who they think they are. Make sure they are being perceived by people who genuinely think they are wonderful because kids always know the truth of what people don't show.

You are responsible for raising a human being to be an adequate an integral part of society. If the other parent is choosing to diminish this then it creates a problem. Everything has the potential for problems. If you love too much it creates problems. If you don't love enough it creates problems. If you control too much it creates other problems. If you don't control enough it creates ginormous problems.

Find the balance. You can't control what the other parent does but you can control what you do and how you allow it to affect you. Make your goal to be the most effective, loving and powerful parent you can be and minimize any ill behavior directed towards you with the necessary force required to maintain your dignity. Keep in mind whatever imbalances the other parent has will only make you stronger. The adversity will force you to stand in your power. If your kids have four different dads or step parents, all of whom are selfish, you are going to have to be mighty powerful. All you can do is de-escalate conflict as much as possible by staying in your power and creating as much love for your kids as possible.

The most powerful person is the one who can stand in adversity and not be affected internally. BE that person, and anyone who tries to undermine you parentally will only be giving you lessons of strength that will teach you to operate even more powerfully. Every time this kind of situation arises, you will again be presented the same choice—either to face the challenge with quiet strength, and resist their attempts to assert control. Or, to capitulate, let them take control, and become an abuser of your children, as well. The choice is determined by who you really are.

How will my child ever start getting good grades?

It's always best to focus on your child's effort and interest, more than the outcome. The grades your child earns are only part of the story. To stress grades above all else means you are focusing on outcomes. When your intention is based in the value of education, you will find yourself focusing on performance, interest, and how excited your child is, about learning. Unfortunately, educational systems in our country are placing more emphasis on test scores and grades than ever before. This is done to tie in with federal funding rules, and other institutional planning. The consequence of this change has been to make education in America become more about competition.

There is nothing wrong with healthy competition. However, it is proven that children learn best when they are relaxed and in a fun environment. Adding extra pressure about the grades will not necessarily improve them. Go to child and ask them what they would like to see happen. Ask them what grade they would like to get. Then ask them what's going on in the class. Maybe there's a good reason why they're getting an "F".

Some of the most intelligent people were freethinkers. They were not designed to regurgitate information given on a test. They were creative. They thought out-of-the-box. There is truly nothing more exciting for someone whose work hard for it, than getting straight A's. Your child may be someone who is focused on other things. Pay attention to their interests. There's always some place in their life they're getting an "A+". Perhaps there are too many emotional problems at home for them to even concentrate on what the teacher is assigning. Investigate and find out the real reason for the slip in education.

Focus on their effort more than the outcome. Tiny adjustments in how you respond can make a big difference. If there is not the pressure there many kids can easily excel. You just have to find the right motivating factor. Bribes have a way of backfiring. Motivational speeches don't last. Find the piece within them that would drive them to want to get good grades. Then use this as leverage. Encourage them. Cheer them on. Be proactive by helping them study and making fun. The number one reason why people fail classes is because the information isn't pertinent for their lives. People are, at that particular stage of their lives, and the information and concepts the teacher wants them to understand.

How do I live the life I want but still have energy to give to my kids?

Support is the most essential factor in being a good parent. When your financial security, in the form of consistent child support or a good job, you can take care of the basic needs. When you have emotional support you can recharge by exchanging emotionally with people who are caring and offer support. When you have mental support you can bounce get feedback on ideas, from other educated people that can help pinpoint where you might be off course or validate what you feel, but may be questioning, because of self-doubt.

Support comes in a variety of forms. Everyone needs a support group to have the life they want. Your support begins with the presence of your significant other; a good solid background in who raised you and people who allow you to be the kind of parent you want to be; and your ability to make decisions that get you to where you want to be.

Getting what we need comes from going out and resourcefully identifying it and then developing the social skills to acquire it. Sitting on the couch in misery or hoping something will change only prolongs suffering. We are all required to be responsible for getting what we need in a way that doesn't destroy other people's quality of living. Setting healthy boundaries helps us meet these needs.

If you came from a family of dysfunction you will have some inner work to do around emotional processing. Parenting is for people who want to see who they are. Parenting is for people who want to love and give of themselves unconditionally. Parenting is for people who want to cultivate a deeper understanding about life and about humanity. Parenting is for people who want to raise children who enhance society. Parenting is for people who have so much love that they want more than just to make a baby. They want to raise a little person. Parenting is for the people who want to do the hardest mental and emotional work they have ever done. No matter who you are as a parent your role is so important. You have to love yourself to even be able to love them completely.

When you are a parent, bring in as many loving people as you can, into the lives of your children. In abusive situations the urge is to retreat to stay safe. The more good people you have in life the better off you and your child will be. This requires a sense of trust—something that isn't easy if you've been hurt. You want a team of people that can help you love your kids and provide fun activities and education for them.

The absolute goal in raising a child is helping assist them in becoming individuals of their own. The more you create a fulfilling life for yourself while loving them, the more potential they have for doing the same because they have had the good fortune of watching an excellent role model. Balance your life. Organize your schedule. And always give them love when they reach for it, no matter what! No matter how busy you are, no matter how many things you need to do, take time to give them the love they need when they are asking for it from you. This is the secret to having the life you want. When you put in the time and give them what they need, then you can feel more comfortable doing your own thing. When you give your children the love they need there will actually be more time for *you* because they will be happy.

How do I keep my sanity in a family that has gone crazy?

Some family members *are* crazy. Who they are and what they do does not make any sense. However, all behavior is rooted in some core psychological issue that serves a purpose. Dealing with family members that behave irrationally has more to do with the love and intention that is in their heart, than anything else.

Some people believe that families have a certain responsibility to stick together. They think that it is disloyal to leave the family. However, some families are ill both mentally and emotionally. The best thing you can do when dealing with a family that seems to have lost its sanity is ask a lot of questions and do your research. You always have a right to choose who you want to be around. You have no obligation to permanently claim them and yet when your heart is open to love you can't help wanting to see them do well. Setting a boundary that protects you while you love them is usually the best answer.

You always have the right to choose who you want to be around. If it is your immediate family that drives you crazy find a new group of people you can call family while still loving your family of origin. If you find yourself feeling depressed for what you don't have with your familial relationships, creativity is the best medicine. People need to see the expression of who they are on the outside of them. When creative impulses go unspoken people get depressed. This is really the biggest problem with family members that are emotionally a wreck; you can't get to where you want to be and feel good. Set boundaries. Let go of any animosity and choose to be around people that allow you to be who you want to be.

I feel vulnerable as a single mother. I wish I could find a good person. How should I handle toxic people that I am dating?

Being a single mom can make you more susceptible to people who are unsafe because you are working as a single operation instead of as a team. Any parent needs good support, but a single parent needs extra support. A single mother should be wary of whose shoulder she turns to in a time of need or desperation.

In times of pain people are more susceptible to what others suggest. If you are not in your power you will feel more vulnerable. Predators prey on people who are vulnerable and needy. When fears of isolation and loneliness are overwhelming people are more likely to put up with control, manipulation and other forms of mistreatment.

Before allowing anyone into your life, consider what type of person would actually be really good for you. Be willing to look at what you might be afraid to see about yourself and about the other person you're potentially dating. If your memories are stuck in an unhealthy pattern you may feel immobilized despite your best efforts.

Control occurs when only one person is allowed to dominate the relationship. Some people think they are supporting you when actually they are controlling you. Make sure you trust your intuition and sixth sense with anyone you come into contact to. Give that same freedom to your children. Honor their sixth sense when they express something.

To really be safe you have to know how to stand your ground and live fully and love and overcome your fear of vulnerability. Learn to develop self-trust, and you will find almost any connection fulfilling. Stay connected to your feelings. Make the best choices based on your feelings in that moment. Pay attention to your feelings so they can guide you to make better choices intuitively.

How do I make more money as a single parent?

There is a formula for making more money when you're already emotionally spent. It comes from eliminating all conflict. The more relaxed you stay as a parent the more centered you are in your earning potential. When you are centered you see opportunities.

Develop yourself in such a way that you are aware of what's going on around you. Be alert to spontaneous opportunities that arise. Consider what you're good at and how you might monetize that talent. There are always ways of making more money. Sometimes we don't have to make more money—we just have to learn how to manage the money we have better.

How do I encourage my child to go out and get a job?

The fundamental problem with teens not working is that so many people 49 become comfortable in life that is financially sedentary. There is something rewarding about working. If they don't have to be proactive in their survival, something inside of them gets stunted. They don't have to grow or become self-actualized.

If we don't learn how to be productive in life we won't thrive. Work is an essential part of life. It is a great way to connect with others through creative exchanging. Unfortunately, many people have lost their gumption to work which is sad because they are missing out on the rewards working brings. People have become greedy and work has lost some of its meaning. Give your child a taste of the satisfaction they can get from working and they will develop a good relationship with the concept of working.

Some people say this country is being run on greed and laziness. The monetary system has been placed in a precarious state by the people controlling our economy. Every day on TV reports show that people are not really working. Talent shows that promise to discover the next huge singing icon, are proliferating on TV. Such influences can easily slant a child's view of work, and what it means. Not everybody wants to do grunt work and in fact many people *can* follow their dreams and make just as much money.

It might be that your child isn't working because they haven't found their passion. Some people have so many of their needs met without effort that the concept of work can become completely foreign to them. If your child is able to go out and work then they will need to learn the skills of exchange within the financial world. At some point you as the parent will need to make peace with their work ethic and let them go. Sooner or later they will figure out they are responsible for their own survival. The quicker that happens, the quicker they will start working.

Everybody has to work and the people who are not working are putting an extra burden on other people that are working. If your children are in the habit of taking, most likely it is because you, the parent, have been too much in a habit of giving. Do your best to encourage and then detach. Let their choices determine what their outcomes are. Eventually if they don't like the outcomes they will make different choices.

Encourage each of your children in a job, then gradually ween them of you, financially. Don't do it suddenly or traumatically. Remember, deep down there is a part of them that wants to work. It gives them freedom, but if they have all the freedom and luxury of home, they will be less motivated to leave.

One of the most important stages of growth as a parenting is learning how to let your child financially soar by letting go. Some parents let go of their kids too soon and make them financially responsible very early on. This can be due to sheer necessity or it can happen because parents think kids need to learn, so they "cut them off" but it builds stress. Anytime you cut children off financially they have to be prepared for it, even if they are 33 years old. You can cause emotional issues to develop around money if you use money as leverage or as a medium for punishment.

The best thing to do to encourage your child to get a job is to emphasize what having a job will do for *them*. If you do this early on—in their teen years—they will naturally develop an attitude that associates work with freedom. People will go out to work when they don't have any money. The most effective way to make your offspring work is to stop giving them any money. If they have to pay for their own gas, wanting to drive might motivate them. If your adult child still refuses to work, that becomes their choice. You can support them in a different way. In a loving and nonjudgmental way, observe the choices they make. Then ask them why? If they answer the question pure in heart you will find there is a good reason for why they are broke, not working, or whatever it may be. They might be in so much emotional pain that they can't bear the thought of getting up and working. You never really know until you ask.

It is up to them to find their own financial power. If you, as parent, assume responsibility for their financial wellbeing, it isn't going to cause them to step into their financial power. It is up to you to find if there is anything you are doing that is not allowing them to step into their power. Give them the freedom and support they need to work with their own creativity. Reward them with praise when they are succeeding. This will do so much more than complaining.

My child was molested and has psychological problems around trust, security and promiscuity as a result? How do I contend with these issues?

Any violation has the probability of diminishing the value of whatever quality was violated. This can be a violation of voice power. This can be a violation of creative power. In this case it was sexual power. However, a sexual violation is so closely linked to the creative energy of self that creative expression gets affected. Depending on the circumstances, one begins to use this creative energy for everything that is sexual. Or, they avoid sexual energy and all aspects of creativity.

A child that has been molested while in your ultimate care has essentially been deprived of the basic need to be protected. This is especially difficult when the one who violates it is the other parent. And yet these things happen. People violate people all of the time because they are disconnected from their own power inside. Abusers end up using people to get the connection they need without thinking about what they are taking. They are selfish, sometimes cruel and in some cases, they are the meanest souls one could ever imagine. Healing from abuse comes from knowing how to tap into your own inner power again that was taken.

If your child was abused it is important for you to maintain equilibrium so you can tend to them. It is interesting in many cases how the abuser seems to get all of the attention for this very reason. They are calm and collected because they had nothing taken.

The focus needs to be on tending to the person who is wounded instead of focusing all of the anger and energy on the one who committed the crime. The anger is completely normal. After all, not only did they cause harm to your precious child's soul, they also just violated you as a parent and your most fundamental role. The anger that rises up is hardwired in order to protect. When an abuser has just circumvented your protection there is a raging fire of anger that comes in to protect the situation even more. The legal system has a way of turning the abuse that is taken out on women and people who have this much anger because the legal system is filled with people who have their own wounds from abuse as well. Always tend first to the person who has been traumatized, then tend to the victimizer, but *only* after everything has stabilized.

The power you will feel after you have processed through your anger will be invigorating. People can heal from anything—even sexual violation—in the healing atmosphere of intimacy, interdependence, and unconditional love that are present within a healthy human family. But know that the healing, itself, can be four to five times more painful than the actual wounding. Like all violations, sexual violations change people. Even if you have been the best parent, your child will now have serious wounds to heal.

The only time a parent can overlook the abuse done to their children is when they have their own wounds that have not been healed. The most important thing in healing any type of wound, that harms your kids, is to remove the defensive behavior that typically develops, in an attempt to protect the trauma. These behaviors are sometimes referred to as masks. Parents develop masks. Children have masks.

The mask that develops in response to any wound is intended to protect the true self. It is an essential defense mechanism. We can develop the social mask that nothing bothers us, when people don't receive our complaints. We can speak and act as though our life were perfect just the way it is, because we are afraid people will reject us if they see that we have problems.

A social mask helps us accomplish what we need to, without being rejected by the group. If your child is not comfortable at home built on a social mask to prevent from people see what's really happening within them. The more you accept wounded children for who they are the more they can let down their guard and *be* who they are. The goal in encouraging a child's happiness is allowing them to be just as they are. A presences mask of denial covers up deeper emotions they would otherwise be expressed no cause a break in a relationship.

We never really know what a person actually went through until they heal. Therefore it is never really fair to judge another person for what they do, not even the abuser. Just be patient with your child. Love them back to their power and they will find their way home inside of themselves again.

How do I have the best relationship with my child?

Home is a significant place in one's life. When you have a home you feel safe, you know you'll survive. People without homes face the extra challenge of staying alive. But, if there's something wrong at home, it impacts every aspect of your life.

If there is a fight at home right before your child is about to go out into the world, it impacts the way they show up in life. The best way to have a great relationship with your child is to have a happy home life.

A great relationship is comprised of all the tiny, memorable moments that add up in life. Take time to be present with your child several times throughout the day and really connect to them and what they have to say. If you spend 15 minutes of quality with them every day, you will have a great relationship with them. In these moments, find out who they are and what they like to do. The more they feel you are really connecting with them, the closer a true affinity they have for you.

This can be observed when a mother who has not dealt with the incest she went through may not see the same thing happening to her daughter. She has a blind spot in her mind because it hasn't been dealt with. A father who was beaten everyday may feel bad reprimanding his child in any way because everything hurt when he was growing up. In turn he has tried to allow nothing to hurt his child by eliminating all consequences, even for poor behavior. There will come a time when you are no longer with your children. They will go off on their own and leave home. These types of departures can come faster than one might expect. The question becomes, did you prepare them?

Parents who are holding on prevent their adult children from moving on. But, children are not born dysfunctional. They'll feel no need to be victims of life, unless you teach them to be. It is parents, themselves, who teach kids how to be powerless. They do this by being too controlling, and they do it by coddling their children, as if they were pets, not human beings.

Kids at any age want to be treated like real people. They like having to work. It makes them feel necessary and effectual. The work has to be given to them, slowly—from age three to four, and onward, so that they are learning all their lives about how they will eventually live as adult human beings. The responsibilities you give to your children must always be appropriate to their age and developmental level. You can't expect a five year old to clean their room perfectly. If they are given too much responsibility at too young an age, then life will feel overwhelming. A child that can't handle life can't leave home at the time when it is appropriate.

By the time teenagers leave home you are in the seventh stage of parenting. One can only hope they are ready to do so. When they go out into the world, they will be sustained only by the wisdom and living skills you have taught them. Whether they leave to enter college or the workplace, you can only hope that they have learned that, at eighteen, their lives are legally their own.

Too many parents simply abandon their kids, at this point, thinking their job of managing them is done. It's not. At this point, it's helpful to think of parenting as more like a 26-mile marathon. You aren't going to finish the last most arduous mile, if that third and final "runner's high" hasn't yet kicked in. Very few people simply don't know how to preserve their endurance for this period, and few even seem to know much about it. Lack of this stage of parental follow through can result in children who launch, but fail. If that happens to your children, you may feel as though you gave them the skills, but did they listen? What are they doing?

To understand what is going on, it is instructive to view this as the period of time when they are your exact mirror. They are going to display to you everything you actually *did* teach them. They will not do this with words, but with behavioral evidence—reflected back to you—of who you were, as a person, when you were teaching them.

If a daughter looks for her mother's approval her whole life she will most likely find herself struggling with the same dilemma in a relationship where her significant other holds the same power over her. A mother does her daughter a huge favor by just accepting her for who she is. Such an easy thing, it would seem, yet is difficult because we are raised in a world that teaches us who we should *not* be. Mothers who critique their daughters are only imparting the wisdom they know that will help them socially.

A father who just accepts his child for who he or she is offers the same value. All rejections are aspects of emotional things the parent has to work through. People are who they are. If a parent doesn't realize when their job is done then it will cause relational friction. A person who is still living out the torment that occurred in their upbringing will overshadow their child's upbringing with these same emotional feelings. All individuals need to be independent. They can still be close to their original family as long as they feel free to be who they are individually.

By the time teenagers leaves home one can only hope they are ready. They are going to have to survive in the world with the skills you have given them. You could send them to college and hope they learn by the time they are eighteen their life is legally their own.

Final Thoughts

People in general want to have a happy inner and outer life. If they have yet to figure this out, they will mostly display defensive behaviors to keep people out. To be a healthy parent you have to work through the emotional hurts that may cause you to keep your guard up. If you have a defensive child, it is often because they don't know how to deal with their feelings that are coming up.

A defensive attitude is nothing more than an indicator that someone doesn't know how to handle then they are dealing with. They are attempting to separate from their emotional pain so they distance themselves with moodiness. People who are defensive are typically opposed to others they fear. Otherwise there wouldn't be a need for an aggressive response. If a person is out of touch with these fears they will use defensive behavior to protect themselves.

Few people are highly evolved enough to articulate what they are feeling while maintaining their power. These same people use defensive behaviors to close off from painful feelings. Defensive behaviors as a parent can be very confusing for a child, which is why it is so important to resolve any inner emotional conflicts.

When there is a plethora of difficult relationships in one's life, the tendency is to either become ultra-independent or helpless. The tendency for both depends on the dynamics of the relationships. A controlling person will demand more emotional bending from the people around them. If a person is not in their own power they will naturally attract a controller that will assume their power.

Power struggles with kids take place all of the time. Power struggles are a natural part of life. Knowing how to stay in your power without becoming controlling is the secret to being an effective parent.

The goal in any healthy relationship is interdependence. Harmony occurs when both parties have the right to be themselves. Both parents and children need this continuous flow that allows each of them to be themselves. The information within this book is built on this premise of mutual respect and honor. Acceptance allows for each person to exchange interpersonal views on what they are both think, feel and experience without having to fear the loss of intimacy.

Loss of connection always comes through rejection. As people learn to be more mindful of their interactions there can be a happier way of parenting. Interdependence always occurs when there is mutual respect and equality. An interdependent attitude will allow for each individual to be honored. The communication and attitude are aspects of true feelings. You will always have a separate personality and different set of needs then the other members in your family yet with interdependence everyone is allowed to be happy and get what they need.

When people are free to be themselves they are operating from a place of interdependence. This is what occurs in the true spirit of emotional intelligence. Take in the information from this book and use it as you will. Many parents have emotional issues inside that prevent them from being the kind of parent they would like to be.

Some of the most effective parenting is intuitive. The answers are all inside of you. When you ask the right questions and always lead with love you find them. Gathering the inner wisdom you need, as you grow, through parenting, is part of the process of raising your own emotional intelligence. Enjoy the process and each stage that comes. You only get to parent your child.

There will come a time when this world won't even be recognized for what it once was. There will be so much love it will be transformed completely.

20 Ways to Raise an Emotionally Intelligent Child

1. Allow your child to listen to their feelings.
2. Trust your own gut feelings.
3. Notice the difference between gut feelings and fears.
4. Strive to be emotionally balanced mentally, emotionally, physically and financially through logical thinking.
5. Take emotional responsibility.
6. Find your inner power to remove yourself from any abusive or toxic situations.
7. Allow each individual to be themselves and individuate.
8. Make your own choices.
9. Allow your children to practice making well-informed choices. Be their teachers, not their rulers.
10. Be appropriately honest about your feelings.
11. Practice kind communication.
12. Set healthy boundaries and limits.
13. Be upfront about your expectations.
14. Remain consistent.
15. Follow-through with your word.
16. Act firmly but with non-violence.
17. See your children through eyes of love.
18. Praise yourself for doing such a good job.
19. Educate your children.
20. Give your children opportunities by providing them with the right encouragement.

Falcons Guards Books are a trademark of a Mountain Lotus Publications Collection. For more information on upcoming classes and events, please visit our website at MountainLotusPublications.com.

For more information about Falcons Guard Centers or to make a contribution to the troubled and homeless youth in this country, please visit FalconsGuardCenter.org.

About the Author

Valerie Harper is a mother of two, a business entrepreneur, and leader in emotional intelligence. She has authored over 32 books on subjects relating to human development, all of which are available through Mountain Lotus Publications, a publishing company that focuses on psychology, science and tacit knowledge.

Her books are also available through Amazon, Kindle and MountainLotusPublications.com. She conducts workshops and trainings in locations throughout the U.S.. These include both educational trainings for professional development and facilitator trainings for parenting and personal development.

Valerie's private consulting firm, Valerie Harper Consulting and True Wealth Consulting, is located in Scottsdale, Arizona, where she resides. He work focuses on personal development, business development, talent development as well as children and families.

For information on her consulting service, or regarding her availability for keynote lectures, teaching courses or developing greater emotional intelligence, Valerie can be contacted through her website, ValerieHarperConsulting.com, or by email at valerieharperconsulting@gmail.com.

Notes

Notes

Notes

Notes

Notes

Notes

Notes

Notes

Notes

Notes

www.ingramcontent.com/pod-product-compliance
Lightning Source LLC
Chambersburg PA
CBHW051928160426
43198CB00012B/2075